WHAT WE BELIEVE
Discovering the Truths of Scripture

Discovery House
P U B L I S H E R S
BOX 3566 • GRAND RAPIDS, MI 49501

PUBLISHING BOOKS THAT FEED
THE SOUL WITH THE WORD OF GOD.

WHAT WE BELIEVE

Discovering the Truths of Scripture

by John F. Walvoord

Library of Congress Cataloging-in-Publication Data

Walvoord, John F.
What we believe: discovering the truths of scripture:
an introductory study of biblical doctrine / by John F. Walvoord.
p. cm.
"Based on the New International Version of the Scriptures."

ISBN 0-929239-31-8

1. Theology, Doctrinal—Popular works. I. Title
BT77.W323 1990   230—dc20   90-35531
CIP

Discovery House Publishers is affiliated with Radio Bible Class,
Grand Rapids, Michigan.

Discovery House books are distributed to the trade by
Thomas Nelson Publishers, Nashville, Tennessee 37214.

Contents

Introduction

As a college freshman I surrendered my life to the Lord and was immediately confronted with questions. What should I make of my life? What did God want me to do? My initial response was that God wanted me to be a missionary, possibly to China. To achieve this goal I decided to complete college and seminary.

It also seemed important that I should learn what the Bible teaches about life, as I recognized it as the Word of God. My mother had given me a Scofield Reference Bible while I was still in high school, and I set myself to read through the Scriptures twice a year. In doing this, I discovered biblical truth as it related to my faith and life.

Later, when graduating from seminary, it became clear to me that God wanted me to dedicate my life to teaching others who were preparing for Christian work, and I accepted a faculty position at Dallas Theological Seminary, where I served for fifty years. I had the joy of seeing thousands of young people, after seminary preparation, going out into the ministry, including many to the foreign field. As I discovered biblical truth through years of study, and passed it on to others, I found that the Bible answers all the important questions concerning this life and the life to come.

From the dawn of history inquisitive humankind has reached for answers to the question of the origin of the world. The Bible reveals that God taught Adam and Eve concerning the divine origin of creation and gave meaning to the order and beauty of nature. But, as the Scriptures reveal, man soon turned from God and divine revelation to find his own answers as embodied in the many false religions that came into existence. As Romans 1:21–32 describes so clearly, idolatry and immorality replaced worship and obedience to God. Then, as now, men forsook the truth and gave themselves to false religion and immorality.

According to the Bible man as originally created was made in the image and likeness of God. As stated in Genesis 1:27, "God created man in his own image, in the image of God he created him; male and female he created them." The history of people as recorded in Scripture reveals that they knew God, that God spoke to them directly, and that He gave them various instructions concerning their life on earth, including the instruction that they were not to eat of the tree of the knowledge of good and evil.

When Adam and Eve sinned by partaking of the forbidden fruit, however, they immediately became conscious of their sin and of their departure from the righteousness of God. As we study the Bible it reveals to us our own sin and the fact that we too have departed from God, but with this we find God's wonderful remedy in salvation. Adam and Eve, having been driven out of the Garden of Eden, faced the sad results of the wreckage that sin brought to the human race. But, for many generations God spoke directly to them, giving them instructions concerning who He was and what He wished them to do. This included the instruction to Abel, Adam and Eve's son, concerning the kind of sacrifice that he was to offer to

God, one in which an animal was killed and blood was shed. As Hebrews 9:22 expresses it, "Without the shedding of blood there is no forgiveness." Although the Bible does not record it, apparently man was also given many moral commands, and because he failed, God had to wipe out the human race with the flood. The Bible is a faithful record of the sin of man and the results it brings. It clearly indicates what our response to the temptation of sin should be and how God can help us obey Him. At the time of the flood God gave specific instructions to Noah concerning the building of the ark in which Noah and his family would be saved when the rest of the world was destroyed by a flood. Communication from God, however, continued, and it is apparent from Scripture that people knew a great deal about God long before the Bible itself was written.

An outstanding illustration of this is the book of Job, which records the life of Job and his problem with suffering and sin. Commenting on Job's problems, his companions stated the many aspects of truth they already knew and some things they had failed to comprehend correctly. The book of Job, however, is so complete in its revelation concerning God and His works that a theology could be written based upon what is stated in that one book. Accordingly, when Abram came on the scene in Genesis 11, humankind already knew a great deal about God and His ways, and Abram received additional important revelation.

Competing with the revelation that came from God were the myths and false religious concepts that were promoted by the devil, even as false religions abound today. These began in the Garden of Eden, where the devil had lied about the Tree of Knowledge of Good and Evil and had told Eve, "You will not surely die" (Gen. 3:4).

This led to Eve's sin and partaking of the fruit. Subsequently, the devil continued his work of spreading false religion and corrupting the human race, which God judged with the flood that cleansed the earth of all humankind except Noah's family. Following the flood, however, the descendants of Noah again were the victims of false religion, which produced the worship of many gods and the creation of many idols. This situation has continued to the present day.

About 1,500 years before Christ, Moses produced the first written Scripture. It served to reveal the truth concerning God and His will for man in an explicit and clear form. Today the Bible in its entirety, the Old and New Testaments, constitutes the revelation of who God is, what His goals and purposes are, and what His rule is for humankind on the earth. Discovering the truth of Scripture is discovering the truth about God.

In Scripture not only does God record history and revelation that relates to history in times past and God's present purpose of salvation in Christ for those who put their trust in Jesus Christ as Savior, but also God reveals the future, from the present into eternity future. Understanding prophecy helps us to prepare for the future that the Bible reveals and teaches us how we can live for eternal values.

About one-fourth of the Bible dealt with the future when it was written. Though many of these prophecies have already been fulfilled, Christians justify their faith in the fact that God knows the future completely. The remaining prophecies are yet to be fulfilled and constitute the important truths about the future. A thorough study of this as provided in the Scriptures will give direction and goals to humankind and will serve to alert all who will heed its admonitions that God is going to judge the world. Eventually God will bring in His eternal kingdom, which will continue forever in the new heaven and the new earth.

The study of prophecy is a fascinating subject and does so much to cast light upon our present path as well as to give the believer in Christ a solid hope for the future. The prophecies of the Bible stand out in sharp contrast to the false prophecies that often characterize false religions. Though there is much in prophecy that can only be partially understood, what is revealed is sufficient to give us clear guidance for our life on earth and our hope for the future.

Questions

1. What is the first question facing a person who wants to do God's will?
2. Does God want everyone to be a foreign missionary? Why?
3. What is the role of the Bible in determining the will of God?
4. What is the role of the Bible in answering questions?
5. What does the Bible reveal about the origin of human sin?
6. What is the place of bloody sacrifice in religion?
7. What are some of the important results of sin?
8. How should we respond to the Bible's revelation of sin?
9. How much did God reveal about Himself before the Bible was written?
10. What did God reveal to Noah?
11. How much does the book of Job reveal about God?
12. Were there early departures from true religious belief?

13. What does the Bible reveal about Satan in the early
     chapters of Genesis?
14. What was added to divine revelation by Moses?
15. Why does one need to study the whole Bible?
16. What is the special benefit of studying prophecy?

How the Bible Was Written

The Bible Is the Source of Christian Faith

ONE OF MY FIRST BIBLE CLASSES in college was a course called Old Testament Introduction. From that class I realized for the first time that the Old Testament was not written in English and, as a matter of fact, was written in an ancient language, Hebrew. As I began to study the various theories about the Bible and the many great thinkers who contradicted its authenticity, I had great difficulty sorting out the truth from error. A wise and competent teacher guided us in the course, however, and it soon became clear to me that the Bible is a wonderful, supernatural book, which is the source of our Christian faith.

Because the Bible is the source of Christian faith, it is very important how we regard the Bible, how we can discover the truths revealed in the Bible, and to what extent we can understand what the Bible teaches.

(1) The Bible is our source of information about God—who He is and what He has done for us. (2) The

Bible is a revelation of man—his character, history, and spiritual needs. (3) The Bible also tells us about God's plan of salvation, which provides forgiveness and renewal for man in his sinful situation. (4) The Bible reveals what God's standards of right and wrong are and what His will is for His creatures. (5) Christian faith is one of hope for the future, and the Bible alone can chart the course of our future into eternity. It would be difficult to overemphasize the importance of the Bible and what it reveals.

The Bible Is an Unusual Book

In a survey of the Bible, one soon discovers that it is a most unusual book and that it has no comparison to any other book that ever was written. Other books on religion are quite different from the Bible. Whether one consults the Hindu Vedas, the Mohammedan Koran, the Confucian Five Classics, or the Jewish Talmud, the Bible clearly stands alone as a comprehensive statement of faith.

Unlike other books, the Bible was written by about forty human authors who lived during a 1,500-year period beginning with Moses in the fifteenth century B.C. The Bible was written in two major languages—Hebrew and Greek, with a few portions of the Old Testament written in Aramaic. No other book has ever been composed in quite the same way as the Bible. The human authors came from various walks of life. Moses, who wrote the first five books of the Old Testament, was probably the best educated man of his day, having studied under tutors in the royal palace of Egypt. The human authors also included those who were great leaders, such as Joshua, and those who were chosen of God to be prophets, such as Samuel, Isaiah, Jeremiah, and Ezekiel. Some of the authors were like David, who began as a shepherd but became king of Israel. From the position of one occupying the throne, he wrote many of the Psalms, forming a rich poetic background for much biblical truth. Some of the writers were farmers; some were warriors; some were fishermen. There was little that tied them together except that they all wrote a portion of the biblical truth as contained in the Bible.

The Bible is an unusual book. In spite of its diversity, it has continuity, beginning in Genesis and ending in the book of Revelation. In its contents are included moral and political law, history, poetry, prophecy, and letters.

In Christian faith the unity of the Bible, in spite of its diversity of subject matter and authorship, is traced to the work of the Holy Spirit rather than to a human penman. The difficulty of producing a book like the Bible can be seen in the fact that if one could choose from all the literature in the world and could select from forty different authors ranging in time for 1,500 years, it would be impossible to create a second Bible equal to what the Bible is itself. Though some have attempted to explain the Bible on naturalistic grounds as simply revision of other current books on religion, the Bible stands as a supernatural production, uniquely different, self-consistent, and presenting a united picture of God and the world.

In the actual writing of the Bible, sometimes the writers had other manuscripts before them that contained facts about the past. The Bible, however, was not a copy of these books. Rather, the authors selected what was true, and the result was a fresh, unique, authoritative word about God's truth.

The Bible Is a Supernatural Book

It would be impossible to explain the origin of the Bible by any other means than to note that it claims to be a supernatural book guided by the Holy Spirit and supports its claim by the facts presented. Though human authors were used and the Bible has clear evidence of their human involvement in writing the Bible, they were so guided by the Holy Spirit that what they wrote was the truth as God wanted it to be said, and they were kept from the error of including anything that was extraneous or unnecessary.

The contents of the Bible make clear that it has to be supernatural in its origin because the Bible includes revelation beyond the scope of people's knowledge. The Bible also presents God's point of view of human activity and history, which would be impossible to learn unless God Himself revealed it.

The Bible is not only supernatural in its origin but also supernatural in its truth, dealing with subjects such as salvation, forgiveness, righteousness, spiritual restoration, and hope for eternity. The scope of the revelation extending from eternity past to eternity future obviously requires divine revelation.

Questions

1. How can we find the truth concerning religion in a world of many conflicting teachings?
2. What are the important facts revealed in the Bible about God?
3. What are the important facts revealed about humankind?
4. What are the important facts revealed about salvation?
5. What important facts are revealed about right and wrong?
6. What important facts are revealed in the Bible concerning God's will for us?
7. What are the important facts revealed in the Bible concerning our hope for the future?

8. In what respect does the Bible differ from other religious books?
9. How was the Bible written and by whom?
10. How do we explain the unity of the Bible with so many different authors?
11. Why do we believe that the Bible is a supernatural book?
12. If you were to summarize what you believe about the Bible, what would be important to you?

[2]

Why Believe the Bible?

THOUGH CHRISTIANS BELIEVE THE BIBLE is the Word of God, it is obvious that the world as a whole does not pay attention to what the Bible says. So why should we pay attention to what the Bible says?

What is Faith?

A nineteenth-century philosopher by the name of Comte held that we should believe only what we can observe personally. Though advanced as a practical philosophy, it is impossible to live with this definition of faith. Everyone in his daily life is constantly believing and acting upon certain facts that are not necessarily proved.

For instance, if we drive a car across a bridge, how do we know by observation that the bridge will not break down? If we board an airplane for a flight to a distant city, how do we know whether the thousands of workers who put the plane together did a good job, whether the mechanics properly checked the plane, whether enough fuel has been added, and whether the flight crew is competent to fly the plane? We have been able to observe none of these factors, and yet we board a plane with a good deal of confidence. In everyday life, faith is a part of the way we live.

But faith is not a totally irrational step. After driving over many bridges and observing others doing the same, we assume that bridges are constructed safely. After flying thousands of miles, we assume that those involved in the process of flying have done their duty well. Though we have only partial knowledge, we believe it is sufficient upon which to base our faith.

In coming to the Bible, we do not have all the proofs that the Bible is the Word of God, but we have many that are quite sufficient. A study of the Bible not only provides an object of faith, something to believe in, but gives us many reasons why we should believe what the Bible states. The answer to why we believe the Bible involves many facts that together provide an intelligent basis for believing the Bible to be a supernatural statement of truth. The Bible itself claims to be a supernatural book that God produced through human authors.

The Bible Inspired of the Holy Spirit

The authors of the Bible do not claim to be men of supernatural knowledge, and they freely admit that God is the source of their information. This is brought out in a central text that states, "All Scripture is God-breathed and is useful for teaching, rebuking, correcting and training in righteousness, so that the man of God may be thoroughly equipped for every good work" (2 Tim. 3:16–17). The claim in this statement is that all Scripture, that is, all the "holy Scriptures" (2 Tim. 3:15), comes from God, who guided the men who wrote it. This was a supernatural process that human minds cannot understand, but the practical effect was that the writers wrote what was their thinking, but their thinking was so guided by God that the very words they used to express the truth were exactly what God wanted them to use.

Because of this, the Scriptures are effective in teaching spiritual truth about God, about morals, about salvation, and about our future hope. The Scriptures are capable of rebuking those who are not obeying its commands. The Scriptures also provide correction. They answer the question, How can a person who is not doing the will of God correct his life and make it correspond to the will of God? They also provide training, or schooling, in righteous living as well as teach all the truth about God, His righteousness, His justification, and the righteousness that He can provide for a Christian. The end result is that the man of God as he studies the Bible will be equipped thoroughly, as the Scripture states, for every good work into which God leads him.

The process of inspiration is beyond our understanding. In reading Scripture, however, it becomes evident that inspiration does not hinder human expressions. As illustrated in many Psalms, the Scriptures record the thinking of the psalmist, even his doubts and his fears. They state his struggles. All of this, however, is by divine design, and what is written accurately portrays the situation and helps one to understand something of the spiritual struggles that every godly person goes through. This also explains how various sources of information can be used sometimes by direct revelation from God, as would be the case in regard to creation and in regard to eternity future or in regard to history as to whether an account of history is accurate or not. Inspiration would assure that God would correct any mistake in recording history and in any other writing that might be used as a basis for information, such as the genealogies and other facts that related to Israel written by the scribes in the Old Testament. In all these cases, inspiration guarantees that what they wrote was accurate and true and that God would supernaturally correct any mistakes that otherwise might appear.

Inspiration does not deter a human author from expressing his own personality and his own vocabulary. For instance, Luke, who wrote the gospel of Luke and the book of Acts, used medical terms because he was a doctor and showed insight into illnesses that other portions of Scripture might not demonstrate. God allowed this but guided him so that what he wrote was exactly what God wanted to be recorded. In other words, even if the author had freedom to express himself, God guided him in such a way that he never expressed what God did not want to be written; he did not leave out anything that God wanted to be recorded; and he did not state anything as true that was, as a matter of fact, not true. In defining the doctrine of inspiration, we may conclude that God supernaturally directed the writers of Scripture without excluding their human intelligence, their individuality, their style of writing, their personal feelings, or other human factors so that His own complete and coherent message to man was written in perfect accuracy with the result that the very words of Scripture bear the authority of divine authorship.

Because the work of inspiration is supernatural, how it was accomplished cannot be completely analyzed, but some help is afforded by the statement of 2 Peter 1:21, "For prophecy never had its origin in the will of man, but men spoke from God as they were carried along by the

Holy Spirit." The figure of speech is of a man in a boat who was traveling to a destination. While he has human freedom within the boat to move around, when the boat arrives, he arrives at the destination. He has been carried by the boat from where he was to where he is going. Likewise, the writers of Scripture, while they had freedom within limits to express themselves, were carried along in such a way that their product was supernatural, and it was the absolute truth, which God wanted them to record in the way and words that He wanted. It is only natural that people attempt to limit the extent of inspiration, and that unbelievers challenge its supernatural character.

In the history of the church various theories of inspiration have arisen. The orthodox position has been that inspiration is verbal and plenary, meaning that it extends to the words and that it is full in its extent. As this was sometimes misrepresented, additional words have been used to describe inspiration; it is not only verbal but infallible and inerrant. In other words, the Bible never affirms to be true something that is actually not true.

In attempting to discuss the issue, some have offered other solutions to the doctrine of inspiration. It has been suggested that inspiration is mechanical, or dictation, and God actually dictated the Scripture. This, however, is not what the Bible teaches, as the Scriptures freely record the author's thoughts, his aspirations, his prayers, and his praise, and other expressions of himself in his human situation. If it were dictated, this would have no meaning and would actually be false. Still another attempt at explaining inspiration is that God gave the concept but the writers were free to express it in their own way. This, obviously, would open the door to many inaccuracies and misunderstandings and is not what the Scripture teaches. It

is very clear in Scripture that the very words of Scripture
are inspired by God.

   Some offer the idea that inspiration is partial, that is,
that it may extend to spiritual truth but not to historic or
geographic matters. This, again, is not what the Bible
teaches and is not an accurate description of inspiration. A
purely naturalistic view of inspiration is, of course, that the
Bible is just a natural book, but this leaves entirely
unexplained the many proofs of its supernatural character
as evidenced in the way it was written and in the extent of
its revelation. In modern times another concept has been
offered. Proponents of this view assert that while the Bible
itself is not inspired, the reader is guided as he reads what
God wants him to understand from the Scriptures. This is
the so-called neoorthodox position. This, however, is
impossible to substantiate, as no two people will come up
with exactly the same concepts, or truths, if they are
allowed to put their personal interpretation on each text.
Accordingly, the only view that the Bible supports and that
really answers the problem of inspiration is the concept
that while the Bible was written by human authors who had
human characteristics, the very words of Scripture were
fully inspired by God, so that they are infallible, that is,
they never will fail, and they are inerrant, that is, they will
never affirm as true something that is false. The statements
of Scripture, however, are subject to proofs, and there are
abundant proofs that what the Bible claims is substantiated
by its contents.

The Testimony of Jesus Concerning
Inspiration of Scripture

   One of the most dynamic and important reasons for
believing in the inspiration of Scripture is that Jesus Christ

affirmed this view again and again. In Matthew 5:18 Christ said, "I tell you the truth, until heaven and earth disappear, not the smallest letter, not the least stroke of a pen, will by any means disappear from the Law until everything is accomplished." In making this statement, Christ is offering the most complete definition of how far inspiration extends. According to Christ, it not only extends to the words but to the letters and even to the smallest part of a letter that would affect the meaning. In the Hebrew, one little stroke, like an English apostrophe, was the letter "yodh." This is the smallest letter. In other cases, simply adding an additional stroke to a letter would change its meaning. This can be illustrated in the English in the capital letter "F." If another horizontal line is added at the bottom of the letter, it becomes "E." This is what Christ meant when He said that the smallest part of a letter has meaning. If this is the case, then the Scriptures as a whole must be true because Christ declared the Scriptures were true to the smallest letter and the smallest part of a letter that would change the meaning. Believing the Scriptures becomes believing the words of Christ Himself.

Many other instances illustrate that Christ affirmed the Scripture. In John 10:35 Jesus said, "The Scripture cannot be broken," which indicates in the context that the very word of Scripture is accurate. In the gospel of Matthew a number of Scriptures are cited, claiming quotations from the Old Testament and affirming the accuracy of Scripture (Matt. 1:22–23; 4:14–16; 8:17; 12:17–21; 15:7–9; 21:4–5, 42). In Matthew 22:29 Jesus asserted that the Sadducees were in error about their denial of resurrection. He stated, "You are in error because you do not know the Scriptures or the power of God." In Matthew 26:31–56 Jesus again asserts that Scripture is being fulfilled accurately. In Matthew 27:9, when Judas took thirty pieces of silver to betray Christ, there is an allusion to Jeremiah 18:1–4 and Jeremiah 19:1–3. Then in Matthew 27:10 Judas used the money to buy a potter's field, foreshadowed in Zechariah 11:12–13. In still another passage, in Matthew 27:35, the gospel writer mentions those who crucified Christ and divided up His clothes by casting lots, alluding to Psalm 22:18 where it states, "They divide my garments among them and cast lots for my clothing." Psalm 22 in its entirety refers to the death of Christ on the cross and contains many allusions to what would be fulfilled when Christ died.

In a similar way, the other gospels as well as the rest of the New Testament consistently support the concept that the Bible is inspired by God and, therefore, is a reliable source of divine revelation.

In His teaching Jesus frequently alluded to the Old Testament and quoted it as a reliable source of information. In Matthew 12:40, for instance, He cites the story of Jonah as an illustration of the fact that He would be in the tomb three days and three nights, putting His stamp of approval on Jonah and its divinely inspired record.

In Matthew 24:15 He talks about "the prophet Daniel" and "the abomination that causes desolation," referring to Daniel 9:27 and Daniel 12:11. Whenever Jesus quoted the Old Testament, even though He was going to add truth to what the Old Testament revealed, He would, nevertheless, affirm the fact that the Old Testament Scriptures were inspired by God.

Though the New Testament was not written while Christ was still on earth, He predicted that the disciples would receive truth from God and would be able to have a supernatural memory concerning the things that happened, as Christ stated in John 16:12–13. The New Testament writers, like those of the Old Testament, were fully aware of the fact that they were being guided by God. In the New Testament 1 Timothy 5:18 quotes Luke 10:7 as equally inspired as the Old Testament passage of Deuteronomy 25:4. Because Christ so completely put His stamp of approval on the Old Testament and predicted that the New Testament would be of God as well, a denial of the written Word of God becomes a denial of the incarnate Word of God.

Internal Evidence for Inspiration of the Bible

Even a casual reading of the Bible will reveal numerous texts where the Bible itself claims to be the Word of God. According to His commands in Deuteronomy, for instance, God says through Moses, "Be sure to keep the commands of the LORD your God and the stipulations and decrees he has given you" (Deut. 6:17). Accordingly, all the instruction preceding and following this passage is equated as a command from God Himself.

An illustration of the power and character of the Word of God is found in Psalm 19:7–11: "The law of the LORD is perfect, reviving the soul. The statutes of the LORD are trustworthy, making wise the simple. The precepts of the LORD are right, giving joy to the heart. The commands of the LORD are radiant, giving light to the eyes. The fear of the LORD is pure, enduring forever. The ordinances of the LORD are sure and altogether righteous. They are more precious than gold, than much pure gold; they are sweeter than honey, than honey from the comb. By them is your servant warned; in keeping them there is great reward."

In this passage the Bible is declared to be perfect, trustworthy, wise, right, radiant, pure, sure, righteous, more precious than gold, sweeter than honey, capable of warning, and greatly rewarding for those who obey it. These qualities do not exist in ordinary literature but characterize the perfection of biblical revelation.

There are many other passages of similar character that in one way or another reflect the Word of God throughout Scripture (Josh. 1:8; 8:32–35; 2 Sam. 22:31; Ps. 1:2; 12:6; 93:5; 119:9, 11, 18, 89–93, 97–100, 104–105, 130; Prov. 30:5–6; Isa. 55:10–11; Jer. 15:16; 23:29; Dan. 10:21; Matt. 5:17–19; 22:29; Mark 13:31; Luke 16:17; John 2:22; 5:24; 10:35; Acts 17:11; Rom. 10:17; 1 Cor. 2:13; Col. 3:16; 1 Thess. 2:13; 2 Tim. 2:15; 3:15–17; 1 Peter 1:23–25; 2 Peter 3:15–16; Rev. 1:2; 22:18). The Bible makes these tremendous claims of being the very Word of God. Thousands of earnest Christians who have examined the Scriptures have found that these claims are fully justified and supportive of all the facts known to us.

External Evidence for the Inspiration of the Bible

The evidences of the inspiration of the Bible are found in many areas, and they serve to support the claims of the internal evidence. One of the important evidences for the inspiration of the Bible is found in the continuity of scriptural revelation from Genesis to Revelation. Though written by different authors, each of them independent as far as their own contribution was concerned, biblical truth and revelation can be traced through book after book, culminating in the book of Revelation. This, obviously, points to the fact that somebody guided the writers so that what they wrote would not contradict previous writers or be a problem to those who followed and that their writings would harmonize with the grand truth being revealed.

Though the authors lived in different times, came from different backgrounds, and spoke different languages, the unity of their presentation is an indisputable evidence for the Bible's inspiration. No other book of multiple authorship can claim what the Bible claims about its unity of revelation.

In its broad sweep of revelation the Scripture also goes far beyond the ingenuity or knowledge of humankind as it speaks of eternity past and eternity future, and it does so with facts that are beyond human investigation. Accordingly, the Scriptures record creation before people were created. The Bible describes the history of the world with prophetic revelation concerning the destiny of human events. Because about a fourth of the Bible was prophetic when it was written and half of these prophecies have been literally fulfilled, it follows that the prophecies relating to events still future will have that same accuracy and literal fulfillment as prophecies in the past. In the light of modern discoveries that are unfolding new aspects of our created world, it is amazing that the Bible, written so long ago, still fits in naturally and intelligently with all the important truths of science that are substantiated and has supernaturally influenced millions of those who have read its pages. No other book has ever been written that has had a wider circulation in more languages, in more cultures, and in more periods of human history than the Bible. Today, as in former years, millions of copies of the Bible are being distributed. As translators reduce languages to writing, the Bible, or portions of it, continues to be translated for the benefit of people of diverse language backgrounds.

The influence of the Bible has not simply been social, though it has affected the morality and spirituality of those with whom it has come in contact, but the Bible has also demonstrated its ability to transform lives. Millions of people read its pages and come to faith in Christ. They testify to the fact of their new birth, a new understanding of the written truth, and a new comprehension of God's plan and purpose for them in the present and in the future.

The influence of the Bible also has in specific ways brought morality and purity of life into focus. The Bible has cleansing power in that its Scriptures point the way to the grace of God and His plan of forgiveness for those who come to Him through faith in Christ. The cleansing aspect of the Scripture was mentioned by Christ in His high priestly prayer at the conclusion of the Upper Room Discourse, "Sanctify them by the truth; your word is truth" (John 17:17). The Bible is the final answer for those who are seeking the answers to the question of what is right and what is wrong. The Bible is also a remarkable piece of literature, embracing such wide subjects, including knowledge about God, knowledge about people, knowledge about human history, knowledge about morality, knowledge about divine purpose, and knowledge about future plans for the human race and the created world. No other book embraces so many different kinds of literature, such as history, theology, poetry, drama, prophecy, and philosophy.

The Bible also deals with the real world, a world of sin and death, a world of divine judgment, and a world of human attainment and human failure. The Bible does not gloss over man's shortcomings, nor does it present the problems without solutions. The Bible is a reliable source of information concerning man's present life as well as the content of his hope in the world to come.

More so than any other book, the Bible exalts Jesus Christ as God's Son, and the constant references to Him in one way or another throughout Scripture provide a portrait of Jesus that no human author could write unaided by the Spirit of God. Throughout Scripture all aspects of Jesus Christ are manifest, including His eternity, His deity, His role as Creator, His incarnation, His future as the Son of David, and His ultimate place of honor in the Godhead. In the gospels Jesus is presented in Matthew as King; in Mark as the servant of the Lord; in Luke as a godly man; and in John as the Son of God. Though the emphasis is different in each of the four gospels, each equally testified to His deity, His humanity, and His possession of the infinite attributes of God. No other book could present so accurately and with such finality the person and work of Jesus Christ as is recorded in Scripture itself.

The Testimony of Fulfilled Prophecy

Though many facts presented in the Bible are not subject to checking or to proof as they depend upon the authority of God and His inspiration of the Scriptures, the Bible also records hundreds of prophecies of the future in a definite and specific way that sets it apart from any other book on religion that attempts to predict the future. As half of the prophecies of the Bible have been fulfilled, it provides a student of Scripture with an accurate insight into how prophecies yet to be fulfilled will be enacted. In the Old Testament the first prophecy of Scripture given to Adam and Eve—that they would die if they chose to eat the forbidden fruit—was literally fulfilled. When they sinned they became sinners who were spiritually dead, and eventually they died physically. The prophecy that God would provide salvation that would crush the head of the serpent (Gen. 3:15) was fulfilled by Christ, who died on the cross for our sins and who ultimately will crush Satan and cast him into the lake of fire (Rev. 20:10). The prediction of the curse on the ground (Gen. 3:17–19) has been literally fulfilled throughout history as man has struggled to provide food for himself and for his family. Throughout Scripture God predicted future events, such as the flood in the time of Noah (Gen. 6–8), an event now history.

Most of the tremendous promises given to Abraham have already been fulfilled. As stated in Genesis 12:1–3, a great nation has come from Abraham; his name is great; he has been a blessing; those who have cursed him have been cursed; and all peoples on earth have been blessed through the death of Christ and His provision of salvation. These great and extensive promises given so long ago are still in the process of being fulfilled.

The record of prophecies and their fulfillment would occupy hundreds of pages if recorded in a book, but each prophecy literally fulfilled is another testimony that when the Bible speaks, it speaks authoritatively and accurately.

In the case of Christ on earth, in His life, death, and resurrection, hundreds of prophecies were fulfilled concerning His person, concerning His attributes, concerning His words, concerning matters of His birth and of His death and of His resurrection. These prophecies have been literally fulfilled and give us intelligent ground for believing that prophecies yet unfulfilled will be fulfilled in God's time.

Problems with the Doctrine of Inspiration of the Bible

Because those who do not desire to submit to the Bible and its claims have sought every possible evidence that the Bible is not true, certain problems have emerged, all of which have been answered satisfactorily by Christian scholars.

One of the common problems is the fact that we do not have the original Scripture writings, and what we call our Bible is a translation from copies of the original. This, at first glance, would seem to introduce an element of error in the Bible as there are thousands of small variations in extant copies of the Bible. However, when these variations are studied, it is found that practically none of them affect the doctrine of Scripture, and that in cases where the teaching of a passage is obscure, other passages that are clear make it evident what the truth of God is. For all practical purposes, the Bible as we have it, even in its translated form, can be used as if it were the very Word of God. Though the original copies of Scripture do not exist, we have many copies of the Old Testament and thousands of copies of portions of the New Testament. As these are compared in what is called "lower criticism," or the attempt to determine the original text, it is possible with great accuracy to determine what the original writings stated.

An illustration of this is the book of Daniel. Until our twentieth century the most recent copy of Daniel came from a period of six hundred years after Christ. In the Dead Sea Scrolls, however, a copy of Daniel was found that was written a hundred years before Christ. As we compare these two versions, recorded some seven hundred years apart, and, undoubtedly, through the pens of many copiers, we find, amazingly, that there is practically no difference. Those who copied the Scriptures did so with such care that any small item that might have crept in becomes irrelevant as far as the truth is concerned.

The same is true of the book of Isaiah. The copy found in the Dead Sea Scrolls was much more ancient than any previous copy and yet it showed practically no variation with later versions. Accordingly, the accusation that we cannot believe the Bible because we do not have the original writings is just as wrong as saying that in a textbook where the Declaration of Independence is recorded we cannot believe it because we do not have the original document in our hands. In any publication small variations creep in, but the variations are so small that we can take for granted that any reputable book quoting an ancient document is doing so accurately. Actually, the Bible is the most accurate ancient writing in existence.

For centuries so-called contradictions in the Bible have been examined. This is especially apparent in the Synoptic Gospels—Matthew, Mark, and Luke—which give parallel accounts of Jesus and the wording is not identical. Scholars have gone over this for centuries, and the result of the best scholarship is the conclusion that no one knows enough to contradict what the Bible says. Because Jesus undoubtedly repeated His messages again and again and many of the statements in Scripture are condensations of much longer messages, it is obvious that the human author is given some freedom in restating the material. The important fact is that the Holy Spirit guided in all of this, and what was written down is absolutely true and reveals God's truth.

An illustration of how problems can be solved may be found in the account of the healing of the blind man at Jericho. In the varying accounts as given in Matthew 20:30, Mark 10:46, and Luke 18:35, the accounts differ as to whether there were two blind men or one. The problem also occurs because in the Synoptic Gospels, Luke 18:35 indicates that Jesus was going into Jericho while Mark 10:46 and Luke 19:1 indicate that He was going out of Jericho. How can such a contradiction be resolved?

Scholars have demonstrated that there were actually three Jerichos. One was the Old Testament Jericho, the other was the New Testament Jericho, and the third was the fort of Jericho. Thus, it would be geographically possible for Christ to go in and out of Jericho three times without retracing His steps. When the further detail of the conversion of Zacchaeus is included in the story, it is obvious that he went back to stay in the home of Zacchaeus. Accordingly, there is no contradiction in that all three accounts are correct. Probably the most profound statement issued by outstanding scholars who believe the Bible to be the Word of God is that no one knows enough to prove that the Bible contradicts itself. The problem is always that we do not have all the information, and if we did, we would understand that what is apparently a contradiction is actually in harmony with the truth.

The Testimony of Faith

For most Christians the various arguments in support of the Bible as the Word of God are unnecessary. Their own contact with Scripture in connection with their conversion to Christianity and their faith in Christ and their subsequent fellowship with Christ is in itself evidence that the Bible is true and that its message can be believed. Such faith, however, does not discard intellectual evidences for the Bible as the Scriptures have abundant evidence that they can be believed as the very Word of God. But there is the confirmation of individual Christians who put their trust in God and found their lives transformed, people who have experienced God's supernatural power as He gives joy and peace through the Holy Spirit. These elements provide truths that are far beyond the ordinary proofs for the inspiration and authority of Scripture. Christians

walking with God find that by meditating on Scripture they
have fellowship with God and that His truth thrills them
and brings them joy and peace in their faith.

Questions

1. To what extent is faith necessary to practical living?
2. How do we exercise faith in our daily lives?
3. To what extent is faith rational?
4. To what extent is faith in the Bible justified?
5. What are some of the facts in the Bible that appeal to
    our faith?
6. What is meant by the inspiration of the Bible?
7. How does the Bible express God's work in inspiration?
8. To what extent does the Bible rebuke, correct, and
    reveal God's will for us?
9. What does the Bible reveal about righteous living and
    the righteousness which God provides?
10. Is there a human element in the Bible relating to the
    authors of the Scriptures?
11. Did the human authors of the Bible often express their
    own personality and feelings?
12. How do you define the inspiration of the Bible in a
    comprehensive way?
13. How would you illustrate the inspiration of the Bible
    by a boat carrying a passenger?
14. What is the orthodox position of the inspiration of the
    Bible?
15. What are some of the wrong definitions of inspiration?
16. To what extent is the truthfulness of the Bible related
    to the truthfulness of Jesus?
17. To what extent did Jesus claim that the Bible was
    inspired?

18. What are some of the statements that Christ made concerning the Bible?
19. What are some of the internal evidences that indicate that the Bible is the inspired Word of God?
20. What are some of the external evidences for the inspiration of the Bible?
21. How does the Bible in its revelation go beyond human ingenuity in the knowledge of man?
22. To what extent has the influence of the Bible been widespread?
23. To what extent does the Bible deal with the real world?
24. To what extent does the Bible exalt Jesus Christ?
25. How does the inspiration of the Bible relate to prophecy in the Bible?
26. Have fulfilled prophecies given us any indication of the truthfulness of the Bible?
27. How can we regard the prophecies of the Bible that are not yet fulfilled?
28. How do we solve the problem that we do not have the original Scriptures or writings?
29. To what extent are our present Bibles identical to those that were written by the original author? What are some illustrations of this?
30. How do we solve apparent contradictions in the gospels?
31. How does Jericho illustrate a method of solving contradictions?
32. How does the experience of Christians in trusting God affect their faith in the Bible?

[3]

The God of the Bible

The Existence of God

THE BIBLE DOES NOT DEBATE the question of whether or not God exists. Rather, the Scriptures present God in the very first verses of Genesis as the Creator, "In the beginning God created the heavens and the earth" (Gen. 1:1). The first and primary evidence for the existence of God is the existence of the creation.

Belief in the existence of God has been a common feature of all races and cultures. The reason for this is explained in the Bible as coming from the creation of man in the image of God, meaning that man would have some capacity for fellowship and communication with God. The Bible also explains that, universally, there is a work of the Holy Spirit in every person testifying to the fact of God's existence.

In the early history of man Scripture testifies that God spoke directly to him, and though there was no written Scripture, that which God revealed was passed down from generation to generation. And in due time man acquired a rather comprehensive view of God as illustrated in the book of Job.

Alongside true revelation of God, however, came the rise of false religions, which the Bible explains as having their source in Satan. Accordingly, the human race departed from its belief in one God and soon began to worship many gods and embodied them in various idols or physical representations. The result was that the whole human race, with few exceptions, departed from God and became the corrupt world that God had to blot out in the flood. It is not surprising, therefore, that today we have many religions that contradict each other, and it is necessary to appeal to the Scriptures to find out what is the true faith.

It is only natural that man, being a reasoning creature, should ask questions about the world in which he lived. Obviously, the world had not been created by man, and yet its design pointed to the fact that someone must have created the world. In our experience, everything shows that intelligent design points to an intelligent designer. For instance, a watch could not just happen; someone had to design and make the watch. Accordingly, there must be a God who is the Creator.

In some ancient religions people worshiped the sun and the moon and the stars, imagining that they were representations of God. The revelation of God in nature is sufficient for the apostle Paul to point out in Romans 1:20 that the world is being judged because of its rejection of the evidence of God in the natural world. Paul said, "For since the creation of the world God's invisible qualities— his eternal power and divine nature—have been clearly seen, being understood from what has been made, so that men are without excuse" (Rom. 1:20). From nature man can learn that God is a person of infinite power and wisdom.

In modern times atheism has appeared with its denial of the existence of God. However, the Bible declares that an atheist is a fool, as stated in Psalm 14:1, "The fool says in his heart, 'There is no God.' " The point is that our world could not have come into existence by accident because it has so many evidences of design and natural law, and all of our reasoning indicates that something cannot show purpose and design apart from a person who thinks and who decides and who has the power to carry out what he thinks. This is why the Bible claims that just from the light of nature people should recognize that God is a person of infinite wisdom and of infinite power because that is what the universe would require to be created.

The Attributes of God

Though much can be learned about God through the study of nature, the Bible goes far beyond this in speaking specifically of the qualities, or attributes, that constitute God. In Scripture God is revealed to be a Spirit, as stated in John 4:24, "God is Spirit, and his worshipers must worship in spirit and in truth." By this is meant that God is not a material being and is immaterial in His essential existence. That God is life is also a major aspect of scriptural revelation. As Christ stated, "For as the Father has life in himself, so he has granted the Son to have life in himself" (John 5:26). The fact that God is life makes it possible for Him to bestow life, that is, eternal life upon those who trust in Christ. The Bible also clearly teaches that God is self-existent. He was not created, but has always existed. In the revelation God gave to Moses, He said, "I AM WHO I AM.

This is what you are to say to the Israelites: 'I AM has sent me to you' " (Ex. 3:14). The concept of self-existence and eternity is contrary to human experience. Any other explanation of God would picture a god who is less than God because it would make God subject to something outside of Himself. Though this cannot be understood, it can be believed because of the infinite nature of God existing from eternity past to eternity future. What is true of His existence is also true of God Himself, that is, God is an infinite Being. The psalmist David said, "Great is the LORD and most worthy of praise; his greatness no one can fathom" (Ps. 145:3).

God is also changeless, or immutable, as many Scriptures testify. In describing God, the psalmist stated, "You remain the same, and your years will never end" (Ps. 102:27). The concept is stated in Malachi 3:6, "I the LORD do not change." It is affirmed of Jesus Christ in Hebrews 13:8, "Jesus Christ is the same yesterday and today and forever."

God is not only the author of truth, but He is truth. Jesus stated in His high priestly prayer the night before His crucifixion, "Now this is eternal life: that they may know you, the only true God, and Jesus Christ, whom you have sent" (John 17:3). Knowing God is knowing the truth. Christ said of Himself, "I am the way and the truth and the life" (John 14:6).

One of the preeminent attributes of God is that God is love, a truth stated many times in Scripture. As stated in 1 John 4:8, "Whoever does not love does not know God, because God is love."

In the nature of being a God who exists from eternity past to eternity future, in His infinity God is also eternal, as stated in Psalm 90:2, "Before the mountains were born and you brought forth the earth and the world, from everlasting to everlasting you are God." If we could imagine a line that extended to infinity in both directions, it would illustrate eternity—time without beginning and without ending.

Another important attribute of God found in many Scriptures is the fact that God is holy, as stated in 1 Peter 1:16, "For it is written: 'Be holy, because I am holy.' " The fact that God is holy leads to the fact that He is righteous and in all His ways He is the ultimate in moral purity. The holiness of God is revealed in Scripture and in salvation, but is not revealed in nature.

Because He is infinite, He also is omnipresent, that is, God is everywhere present. In Psalm 139 the psalmist points out that it is impossible to go anywhere where God is not present. He states, "Where can I go from your Spirit? Where can I flee from your presence? If I go up to the heavens, you are there; if I make my bed in the depths, you are there. If I rise on the wings of the dawn, if I settle on the far side of the sea, even there your hand will guide me, your right hand will hold me fast" (Ps. 139:7–9). Not only is God everywhere present, but He also is personally present and indwells every believer. As stated in 1 Corinthians 6:19, "Do you not know that your body is a temple of the Holy Spirit, who is in you, whom you have received from God?" A Christian is indwelt by all three Persons of the Trinity (John 14:15–17, 23). Just as God is infinite in other attributes, so He is also infinite in His knowledge and is thus omniscient. This is stated in Psalm 147:5, "Great is our Lord and mighty in power; his understanding has no limit."

In keeping with His infinity, God is also omnipotent, or all-powerful. This means that He can do all He wills to do. As stated in Matthew 19:26, "With God all things are possible." But God will not lie or be untrue to His nature. He always wills to do what is in keeping with His perfect nature. Other qualities can be added that are not considered formal attributes, such as the fact that God is good, merciful, sovereign, and that His works are perfect. Everything that is true of God is true of God to infinity. It sets Him apart from anything that God has created.

God the Father

In Scripture God is described as a Trinity—God the Father, God the Son, and God the Holy Spirit. In theology God the Father is called the First Person of the Trinity because in the nature of the relationship of the Father, Son, and Holy Spirit, the Father sends the Son and the Spirit, rather than the Son sending the Father. As Father, He is Father over all creation. He is Father in the sense that He is the originator of everything that has been made. In Malachi 2:10, for instance, the questions are asked, "Have we not all one Father? Did not one God create us?" In the sense that God the Father is our Creator, it is proper to speak of the universal fatherhood of God. This must not be understood, however, in the sense that all men are the spiritual children of God because this is true only of those who are born again, and the universal fatherhood of God does not bring with it any sense of salvation for all men as some have taught.

In the Old Testament God was also the father of Israel in that he established a relationship wherein He had a special place for Israel in His plan for humankind. In keeping with this, Moses told Pharaoh in Exodus 4:22, "This is what the LORD says: Israel is my firstborn son, and I told you, 'Let my son go, so he may worship me.' But you refused to let him go; so I will kill your firstborn son."

As in the universal fatherhood of God, the special Sonship that Israel enjoyed did not assure to them individual salvation but did assure to them the promises that God had made to the nation as such.

God is also revealed in Scripture as the Father of our Lord Jesus Christ, as stated in Ephesians 1:3. Though the father and son relationship is not the same as human fathers and sons in that Jesus existed from eternity past as well as God the Father, it does indicate a relationship where the Son accomplishes a work on earth on behalf of the Father. This is embodied in the familiar text of John 3:16, where it says that God, that is, God the Father, gave His Son to provide a Savior for humanity. Accordingly, while the Scriptures are clear that God is the Father of Jesus Christ, the Son is not subsequent to, inferior to, or in any way less God than God the Father. As the Father of the Lord Jesus Christ, God has a peculiar relationship to Him that differs from His relationship to any other person. In John 3:16 the Son is referred to as "his one and only Son," or, literally, "His only begotten Son." Likewise, in other passages, such as Colossians 1:15, He is declared to be "the image of the invisible God, the firstborn over all creation." Firstborn does not indicate that He was born in His deity but that He was firstborn in the sense that He was before anything that was created, being eternal like God the Father.

A final aspect of the fatherhood of God is that He is the Father of all who believe in Christ as Savior. This is based upon spiritual birth, not natural birth, but it pictures the believer as belonging to the family of God in which God is Christ's Father. As believers in Christ, they are declared to be "children of God—children born not of natural descent, nor of human decision or a husband's will, but born of God" (John 1:12–13). This is affirmed in Galatians 3:26, "You are all sons of God through faith in Christ Jesus." That God is the Heavenly Father of believers in Christ leads to the wonderful truth that as the sons of God, Christians are heirs of God and joint heirs with Christ (John 1:12–13; 3:3–6; Rom. 8:16–17; Titus 3:4–7; 1 Peter 1:4). The Fatherhood of God is, accordingly, an important aspect of Christian faith and is supported by many Scriptures (John 20:17; 1 Cor. 15:24; Eph. 1:3; 2:18; 4:6; Col. 1:12–13; 1 Peter 1:3; 1 John 1:3; 2:1, 22; 3:1). The fact that God is our Father, a God who is infinitely loving, gracious, powerful, and all-wise is a comfort to believers as they seek to find the Lord's will for their life and understand the meaning of spiritual experience.

As a small boy I thought my father was the most wonderful person in the world. Whenever I brought him a problem, he seemed to solve it so easily. I could always be assured of his love and care.

On one occasion I asked my father why he was not President of the United States. To me, this was the best job, and my father ought to be President. I will never forget how my father, rather embarrassed, attempted to explain to me why he was not President. Our Heavenly Father, however, is worthy of all worship and praise and is everything a father could be, infinitely loving, infinitely wise, infinitely patient, infinitely resourceful, and able to do anything He wills to do.

God the Son

Jesus Christ is unquestionably the central object of Christian faith. Most Christians came to Christ because they heard the gospel message that Jesus Christ, God's Son, had died on the cross for their sins and rose again.

Accordingly, their introduction to biblical truth and their introduction to God is through knowledge and fellowship with Jesus Christ.

Because Jesus Christ is the center of our faith and Christianity gets its name from Christ, it is most important that we understand who He is and what our relationship to Him is.

Scriptures are clear that as the eternal Son of God He is God in all that this term means and that He has existed from eternity past and will continue to exist to eternity future. Though Christ is introduced to most observers in connection with His life on earth when He became man, it is also clear that He existed long before He was born.

Like other members of the Godhead, Jesus Christ existed from all eternity past. This is stated in John 1:1–2, "In the beginning was the Word, and the Word was with God, and the Word was God. He was with God in the beginning." Just as Jesus is eternal, it is obvious that He is also God, and Scriptures are abundant in their testimony to this. In fact, the whole gospel of John was written especially to bring men to faith in Christ. In John 20:30–31 the truth is revealed, "Jesus did many other miraculous signs in the presence of his disciples, which are not recorded in this book. But these are written that you may believe that Jesus is the Christ, the Son of God, and that by believing you may have life in His name." The Bible not only states in many passages that Jesus Christ is God but also supports this fact by the many miracles that He performed in His life on earth. The fact that He was able to raise Himself from the dead is the ultimate proof that He is, indeed, all that He claimed to be—God's eternal Son.

Many other direct statements relate to His eternity and deity. In Isaiah 7:14 His virgin birth was announced, and He was given the name "Immanuel," meaning "God with us." In Isaiah 9:6–7, referring to the birth of Christ, He is called "Mighty God." Jesus' own statement in John 8:58 that He was "before Abraham was born" was correctly understood by the Jews as claiming that He was the eternal God. Jesus Himself referred to the fact that He existed before the world was created. In John 17:5 Jesus said, "And now, Father, glorify me in your presence with the glory I had with you before the world began." Philippians 2:6–7 also refers to Christ as existing long before His incarnation; and Colossians 1:15–17 makes a very specific claim concerning Christ, "He is the image of the invisible God, the firstborn over all creation. For by him all things were created: things in heaven and on earth, visible and invisible, whether thrones or powers or rulers or authorities; all things were created by him and for him. He is before all things, and in him all things hold together." Christ is said to be the Creator and the "exact representation" of God. So many biblical references support the deity of the Son of God that anyone who accepts the accuracy of biblical revelation also accepts the deity of Christ.

In addition to the direct statements, there are many implications that support the concept that Christ is the Son of God. For instance, in the Old Testament He appeared as the angel of the LORD (Gen. 16:7; 18:1; 22:11–12 and many other references). He no longer appears as the angel of Jehovah once He becomes incarnate in the New Testament. Many titles are also ascribed to Christ, including the term "God with us," "the Son of God," "the first and the last," "Lord of all," "Mighty God," and "God blessed forever." Such titles and many others could not be ascribed to Him if He were not actually the eternal Son of God.

In the New Testament Jesus is constantly associated with the Father and the Holy Spirit as equals (Matt. 28:19; John 14:1; 17:3). Because Christ has all the attributes of God, he must necessarily be God Himself. In the worship of Christ as God and in the obedience to Him as Lord, there is constant recognition that He is God and all that this implies.

In the Incarnation when Jesus was born of Mary the new situation included that Jesus had in addition to His divine nature a complete human nature composed of soul, spirit, and body. The fact of the Incarnation is one of the well-attested events of the Bible and is supported throughout the Bible, but particularly through the four gospels, as well as in both Old Testament prophecy and New Testament fulfillment. In the Old Testament Christ is constantly represented as a man who would die for the sins of the world, as illustrated in Isaiah 53. All the typology of offering a lamb as a sacrifice for sin in the Old Testament looked forward to the Lamb of God who would take away the sin of the world (John 1:29). The life of Christ on earth demonstrated beyond any question that He was a man. His humanity is again revealed in the fact that He died and was resurrected. As the God-Man He is now in heaven at the right hand of God the Father. Though the addition of a complete human nature was a dramatic change in the person of Christ, it did not alter in any way the fact that He was also all that God was.

God the Holy Spirit

From Genesis 1:2 to Revelation 22:17, the Bible records constant references to the Holy Spirit—His person and His work. Like the Father and the Son, He has all the attributes of the Godhead and is especially active in the world scene. Pharaoh saw in Joseph the working of the Spirit (Gen. 41:38).

The Holy Spirit was not only the source of spiritual power but also was related to skills in various fields of work. For instance, Bezalel, according to Scripture, was filled with the Spirit of God, who gave him "skill, ability and knowledge in all kinds of crafts" (Ex. 31:2–3). He was able to work in gold, silver, bronze, cut stone, and wood and work with other types of craftsmanship. Other workers in the temple were also given supernatural skill to produce the tabernacle.

The Holy Spirit also gave men qualities of leadership, as in the case of Joshua. The Lord said to Moses, "Take Joshua son of Nun, a man in whom is the spirit, and lay your hand on him" (Num. 27:18). In the encouragement given to Zerubbabel in connection with building the temple, he was told, "This is the word of the LORD to Zerubbabel: 'Not by might nor by power, but by my Spirit,' says the LORD Almighty" (Zech. 4:6).

In the New Testament the Holy Spirit takes on even more significance than in the Old Testament for He is seen in the miracles of Christ, He descends on the day of Pentecost to indwell every believer, and throughout the present age He works in and through believers to accomplish the work of God. In many respects, the relation of a believing Christian to God is a relationship of fellowship with the Holy Spirit in which the Holy Spirit empowers and enables the individual to lead a life that glorifies God. Though He is the "Sent One" by both Christ and the Father, He nevertheless is equal with them in power and glory and has all the same attributes that belong properly to deity.

The Unity of the Trinity

In contrast to the polytheism of the heathen world with its many gods and idols, the Christian faith centers in one God. This God, however, is revealed to be a Trinity, including the Father and the Son and the Holy Spirit. As such, we distinguish the Father from the Son and both of them from the Holy Spirit. Though described as three persons, they are not three persons in the sense of three individuals, but rather constitute one God. As stated in Deuteronomy 6:4, "The LORD our God, the LORD is one." In the Hebrew the word "LORD" is *Yahweh*, or Jehovah, meaning "I AM," the most sacred name of God in the Old Testament and used only with the God of Israel. The word "God," however, "our Elohim," is plural referring to the plurality of God and implying the Trinity. Thus Jehovah, the one God who is also Elohim, the three persons, is one Lord, preserving the unity of the Trinity.

All students of scriptural truth labor to understand the doctrine of the Trinity, but it eludes them because it is beyond anything that they experience in this life. There is really no illustration of the Trinity though a musical chord may combine several notes, and a beam of light may combine several colors. But this is not clearly parallel to the Trinity. Accordingly, the best procedure is to accept the Bible as true and accept the fact that there is one God who exists in three persons and leave the explanation of this to the life after this.

The fact that there are three persons in the Trinity is stressed throughout the Scriptures, particularly in the New Testament, and there can be little doubt that this is what the Bible teaches. For instance, in Matthew 3:16–17 the record is given of Jesus' baptism, where there was a voice from heaven saying, "This is my Son, whom I love; with him I am well pleased" (Matt. 3:17). At the same time, while God the Father was in heaven, the Holy Spirit was descending like a dove and lighting on Christ (Matt. 3:16), and Christ Himself was being baptized. Accordingly, all three persons of the Trinity exist as three persons who are also one. The fact of the Trinity is supported by the baptismal formula mentioned by Christ where He instructed His disciples to "go and make disciples of all nations, baptizing them in the name of the Father and of the Son and of the Holy Spirit" (Matt. 28:19).

The doctrine of the Trinity affirms that there are three persons in the Godhead who are one. However, the members of the Trinity are distinguishable by having certain properties that differ even though they are equal in attributes. Therefore, the first Person is called the Father, the second Person is called the Son, and the third Person is called the Holy Spirit. There is obviously no parallel to this in human experience, and accordingly, the doctrine must be accepted by faith. On the one hand, we should avoid the idea that they are three separate persons, like Peter, James, and John. On the other hand, we must avoid the idea that they are just modes of existence of one person. The doctrine of the Trinity, therefore, presents God as a unique God who differs from all heathen gods as such and is the consistent presentation of the nature of God in the Bible.

The Sovereignty of God

The fact that God possesses all the infinite attributes that characterize God makes plain that humankind is the object of His creation, and as creatures, they should worship their infinitely divine Creator. Because God is who He is, He obviously has the right to control and command His creatures and to judge them if they disobey.

By believing in God we recognize that as God He has a right to direct our lives. One of the supreme tests of our faith is whether we are willing to submit to the will of God for our lives and do the things that please Him.

In spite of the sovereignty of God, it is clear that God has given to man certain freedoms, especially in the area of moral choice. Though there are no surprises to God and He is never uncertain about the outcome of any human event, it is, nevertheless, true that man is responsible for what he decides even if God anticipated his decision before it took place. Accordingly, it is necessary for man to put his trust in Christ to be saved (Acts 16:31). The fact that God knows in advance whether some will accept Christ and others will not does not change the validity of this choice. It is also true that God, to some extent, works in human hearts to accomplish His will (Phil. 2:13), but this never goes to the extent that God forces a person to accept Christ as Savior or forces him to surrender his life to the Lord. It is, rather, as is indicated in Romans 12:1–2, a matter of urging us to present our lives a living sacrifice in view of God's mercies to us. In 2 Corinthians 5:14 the same thought is embodied in the statement, "For Christ's love compels us, because we are convinced that one died for all, and therefore all died." Even though God has permitted humankind to choose his way, whether good or evil, it is nevertheless true that His sovereignty maintains control, and in the end every righteous act will be rewarded and every wicked act will be punished.

Questions

1. How do the Scriptures present the existence of God?
2. How does the fact of creation introduce God?
3. How did people accumulate knowledge about God before the Bible was written?

4. How did false religions arise? How do we answer
   false religions today?
5. What does creation as a whole reveal about God?
6. How does a watch illustrate intelligent design?
7. To what extent does the Holy Spirit reveal the fact of
   God's existence?
8. To what extent does the revelation of God in nature
   provide a sufficient basis for faith so that the world is
   judged because it rejects this evidence?
9. Why is an atheist a fool?
10. What is meant by the idea that God is a Spirit?
11. How does the Bible refer to God as self-existent?
12. How does the Bible refer to God as changeless or
    immutable?
13. How is God the author of truth and truth itself?
14. Why does the Bible reveal that God is love?
15. How does the revelation of God as love provide a fact
    not found in the natural world?
16. How does the Bible reveal that God is holy? And how
    does this contrast to revelation in the natural world?
17. What is meant by the idea that God is omnipresent?
18. What is the difference between God being omnipresent
    and being personally present, indwelling every
    believer?
19. What is meant by the attribute of omnipotence?
    How would you define the omnipotence of God in
    relation to His will?
20. Does the omnipotence of God permit Him to lie or to
    do anything that is contrary to His nature?
21. What are some other qualities of God that usually are
    not considered formal attributes?
22. What do we mean by the doctrine of the Trinity?
23. Why is the first person of the Trinity called the Father?

In what sense is He Father in relation to creation?

24. Does God as the Father of creation justify the idea that everyone is a child of God?

25. How is God Father in relation to Israel?

26. How is God Father in relation to Jesus Christ?

27. In what sense is God the Father of believers in Christ?

28. To what extent is our Heavenly Father able to meet our needs?

29. To what extent is Jesus Christ as God's Son the central object of our faith?

30. What leads to the conclusion that Jesus Christ as the Son of God existed as such long before He became a man?

31. What are some of the reasons for believing in the eternity of Christ?

32. What are some of the reasons for believing in the deity of Christ?

33. What do we learn about Christ as the Creator?

34. What was the new situation regarding Jesus Christ when He became a man?

35. Did the Incarnation, when Jesus became a man, change His deity?

36. What are evidences that Jesus Christ was a genuine human being even though He was God?

37. What are some of the early evidences of the power and ministry of the Holy Spirit in the Bible?

38. How is the Spirit of God related to ability in various areas?

39. How is the Spirit of God related to leadership?

40. How is the Spirit of God related to power?

41. What did the Spirit of God do on the Day of Pentecost?

42. How do we define God as a unity even though He is a trinity?

43. Why is the doctrine of the Trinity beyond our complete comprehension?

44. How is the doctrine of the Trinity supported by the baptism of Jesus?

45. How do we justify the term "first Person" in relation to the Father, "second Person" in relation to the Son, and "third Person" in relation to the Holy Spirit?

46. How does God as sovereign have the right to control and command His creatures?

47. How does the sovereignty of God relate to a Christian attempting to live in the will of God?

48. To what extent do people have choices in the moral realm?

49. To what extent does God influence a Christian to do the right thing?

50. What fundamental truth is stated in Romans 12:1–2?

51. How does the love of Christ compel us?

[4]

The Human Race: Its Creation, History, and Destiny

The Creation of Man

HOW DID THE HUMAN RACE BEGIN? The Scriptures introduce man as a created being. In Genesis 1:27 this truth is stated, "So God created man in his own image, in the image of God he created him; male and female he created them." The origin of man has long been the subject of human speculation. But in spite of all that has been done scientifically and otherwise, no one has ever come up with a better explanation than creation for the origin of man.

In recent centuries the theory of evolution has arisen, which attempts to explain all species of life, whether plant or animal, as a product of a gradual improvement that develops over many millions of years. The problem with evolution, however, is that it is a theory that has yet to be proved. With all the advantages of modern science, it has never been possible to change one species into another; a dog never becomes a cat; a plant never becomes a fish; and a tree never becomes a cow. In other words, a tree remains a tree though it may vary in its structure and leaf design and new kinds of trees can be formed, but the fact is that we have never been able by any scientific process to change one species into another.

Evolution has no solution for the origin of life. Science never has been able to produce life out of that which was not life. The Bible remains the simple and effective and clear explanation of how man was created. Further, in the creation of man he was made in the image and likeness of God (Gen. 1:27). No development in evolution could ever take an animal and produce in it that which corresponds to the image of God.

The revelation that man is the object of God's creation is not simply taught in one passage but in many. In the first chapter of Genesis alone the fact of man's creation is stated repeatedly. In the sweeping statement of John 1:2–3, Jesus Christ as the Word was "with God in the beginning. Through Him all things were made; without him nothing was made that has been made." Colossians 1:16 is even more explicit, "For by him all things were created: things in heaven and on earth, visible and invisible, whether thrones or powers or rulers or authorities; all things were created by him and for him."

According to Hebrews 11:3, all things, not simply human beings, were made by God: "By faith we understand that the universe was formed at God's command, so that what is seen was not made out of what was visible." If one accepts the Bible as the Word of God in other matters, one must necessarily accept the Bible when it indicates that God is the Creator and originator of all that has been created. It is significant that even unbelievers who scoff at the second coming of Christ have to conclude, "Ever since our fathers died, everything goes on as it has since the beginning of creation" (2 Peter 3:4), in other words, they must begin with creation. There is no alternative explanation to the doctrine of creation that satisfies the questions that are raised by the nature of our universe and the nature of man.

The Nature of Man

In the original creation as stated in Genesis 1:27, man was made in the image and likeness of God. This means that he has the essential qualities of personality, which are intellect or mind, sensibility or feeling, and will, that is, the ability to make moral choices. These qualities do not exist in any creature other than man, but they make it possible for him to have communion with God and also to be morally responsible for his actions.

The Scriptures further define man as composed of that which is material or immaterial. Accordingly, man has a body and he has life. In considering the matter of the life of man, the Scriptures record, "The LORD God formed the man from the dust of the ground and breathed into his nostrils the breath of life, and the man became a living being" (Gen. 2:7). As man is discussed in Scripture, it becomes evident that in addition to material and immaterial, the immaterial part of man is considered under two major aspects—that of spirit and soul. When man was created, according to Genesis 2:7, he "became a living being," literally, man became "a living soul" (KJV). Several hundred times in both the Old and New Testaments man is declared to possess a soul.

The Bible also claims that human beings possess a spirit. In Hebrews 4:12 the Word of God is said to penetrate human consciousness to the point that "it penetrates even to dividing soul and spirit." In general, the word "soul" seems to refer to the psychological aspect of man or his natural experience of life. The word "spirit" seems rather to refer to his God-consciousness and his ability to function in moral and spiritual realms. However, in the Bible these terms are sometimes used to refer to the whole man, such as the words "body" or "soul" or "spirit." For instance, in Romans 12:1 believers are exhorted to offer their bodies as living sacrifices to God. In referring to a believer's body, Paul is referring to the whole person. Likewise, "soul" sometimes refers to the whole person, and sometimes "spirit" refers to the whole person.

Other immaterial aspects of man are also mentioned in the Bible, such as mind, will, conscience, and other references to aspects of human personality. While the body of a Christian is considered sinful, it, nevertheless, is referred to in Scripture as the "temple of the Holy Spirit" (1 Cor. 6:19). The bodies of Christians should be kept under control and made to submit to the human mind (1 Cor. 9:27). The bodies of Christians, which now are corrupt and sinful, are going to be transformed, cleansed from sin, and made new like the resurrection body of Christ, at the time of resurrection or rapture (Rom. 8:11, 17–18, 23; 1 Cor. 6:13–20; Phil. 3:20–21). Though man in his present humanity is sinful and comes short of what God would have him to be and do, Christians can look forward to the time when their bodies will be made perfect in the presence of God.

The Problem of Sin

The problem of sin in the world has been faced by theologians as well as by philosophers of all kinds, and some explanations have been attempted. People who ignore the Bible fall into two classifications—those who explain sin as that which occurs because God is not omnipotent and could not prevent it, and those who postulate that God Himself is sinful and that, therefore, sin is in the universe. Adherents to polytheism, the belief that there are many gods, assume that the gods have limitations, that they are not omnipotent, that they sin. Therefore, they can offer no solution for the sin problem.

Christianity explains the problem in terms of divine revelation and what took place after Adam and Eve were created. The answer to the sin problem is that man freely chose evil and this brought sin into the human race. God had commanded Adam and Eve, "You are free to eat from any tree in the garden; but you must not eat from the tree of the knowledge of good and evil, for when you eat of it you will surely die" (Gen. 2:16–17). The biblical narrative in Genesis, however, continues with the account of how Eve partook of the fruit of the tree and Adam joined with her in partaking of it (Gen. 3:2–6). The result was that the entire human race was plunged into sin.

The biblical narrative also supplies the fact that Satan, who appeared to Eve in the form of a serpent, was evil. This implies that there was an original creation of the angelic world and that some of the angels sinned against God and became the demon world, led by Satan, that exists today. Scripture assumes that God would not create evil but created a world in which there was moral choice possible, and both angels and men chose evil instead of that which was right.

Unlike the philosophic world, which has no solution for the problem of evil, the Bible not only accounts for its origin but also provides a divine remedy in the promise of Genesis 3:15 that the woman would have offspring who would crush the head of the serpent, fulfilled in the death of Christ on the cross and His resurrection. Satan was defeated and his ultimate judgment was assured.

A biblical doctrine of sin is absolutely essential to understanding the Scriptures as an account of God's revelation of salvation that is available through Christ and a record of victory over sin that is promised to those who will put their trust in God. The doctrine of sin is at the root of explaining history with its record of wickedness, suffering, sin, and death. The proper doctrine of sin is also necessary to understand humankind and his reaction to God and to God's revelation.

Before Adam sinned he was innocent in thought, word, and deed. He had been created without sin but with moral choice. The challenge of obedience to God was very simple. The only command God gave that could be disobeyed was the command not to partake of the forbidden fruit (Gen. 2:17).

After Adam sinned a radical change took place. He died spiritually. Physical aging began the process that led ultimately to his death, and his conscience was aware of the fact that he had sinned against God. The immediate result of sin was that God cursed the serpent for tempting Eve (Gen. 3:14–15). The woman was promised that she would be subject to her husband and that her pain in childbearing would increase (Gen. 3:16). Adam was promised that the ground would be cursed because of him and he would find it difficult to produce food. He was also informed that eventually he would die and return to the dust from which he was made. Because of the changed situation, Adam and Eve were driven out of the garden where they had been placed, which prevented them from eating of the Tree of Life, which would have given them physical life forever (Gen. 3:22–24).

The Effect of the Fall on the Human Race

The devastating effect upon Adam's personal situation was extended to the entire human race because Adam was the head, or beginner, of humanity.

In the discussion of sin and its effect upon the human race, the Bible teaches that what Adam did was imputed, or reckoned, to all his descendants. Accordingly, it is revealed in Romans 5:12–14:

> Therefore, just as sin entered the world through one man, and death through sin, and in this way death came to all men, because all sinned—for before the law was given, sin was in the world. But sin is not taken into account when there is no law. Nevertheless, death reigned from the time of Adam to the time of Moses, even over those who did not sin by breaking a command, as did Adam, who was a pattern of the one to come.

The whole human race was considered as if they themselves had done what Adam did, and the judgment was affirmed that if they had the same opportunity in the same situation that they would have sinned against God also.

In providing a solution for human sin as intimated in Genesis 3:15, God provided in Christ crucified the One who would make it possible for people to be saved. This required an imputation, or a reckoning, of people's sin as if Christ Himself had performed it. As stated in 2 Corinthians 5:21, "God made him [Christ] who had no sin to be sin for us, so that in him we might become the righteousness of God." When Christ died on the cross, He died in our place as a Lamb of sacrifice because He was bearing the sins of the whole world (John 1:29).

The fact that Christ has died and paid the price of man's sin makes it possible now for God to reckon, or impute, righteousness to those who believe in Christ. An earlier example of this is the statement that when Abram believed in the Lord concerning his future posterity, "it was credited to him as righteousness" (Rom. 4:3). Accordingly, though Abram was a sinner like all other members of the human race, when he put his trust in God as the one who would fulfill His promises, he received by divine reckoning the righteousness that only God can give. Accordingly, the same God who permitted sin to occur also provided a Savior in the person and work of Jesus Christ, which now makes it possible for sinners to be saved and be considered righteous in God's sight.

The principle of imputation of righteousness to those who believe in Christ is the basis for our justification and is mentioned frequently in Scripture (Rom. 3:22; 4:3, 8, 21–25; 2 Cor. 5:21; Philem. 17–18). Though it is difficult to understand completely what Christ did when He died, He died as our sin-bearer, as the Lamb of God who takes away the sin of the world, a fact that is mentioned many times in Scripture (Isa. 53:5; John 1:29; 1 Peter 2:24; 3:18). The fact that Christians have been made righteous and justified before a holy God makes it possible for them to be a part of the body of Christ through the baptism of the Holy Spirit (1 Cor. 12:13).

Just as the Scriptures make clear that a believer in Christ is justified by faith, or declared righteous in the sight of a holy God, so it is also true in Scripture that one outside of Christ has none of the benefits of Christ's redemption. The unsaved have the sin of Adam reckoned to their account; they are born with a sin nature that naturally sins against God; and to this their personal sins are added. Because of Adam's sin everyone, even those who are Christians, experiences physical death (Rom. 5:12–14).

Those who are not saved through faith in Christ are spiritually dead and are separated from God (Eph. 2:1; 4:18–19). They will also experience the second death, which is defined as eternal separation from God (Rev. 2:11; 20:6, 14; 21:8).

The History of Man

The history of man since Adam and Eve brought sin into the world has been a sad record of the human race departing from God in spite of all that God has done for them. Though Adam and Eve had consciences that enabled them to distinguish right from wrong, that did not make them good, and their posterity drifted farther and farther from God until God decided to destroy the whole human race, except Noah and his family (Gen. 6:13). Following the flood, God gave to Noah the basic principles of human government. However, the human race again demonstrated its depravity by building the Tower of Babel, and God had to judge by confusing the languages of the people.

With almost the entire world departing from God and sinning flagrantly, God chose Abram to fulfill His purpose in redemption. To Abram was promised that he would be able to bring blessing to the entire world (Gen. 12:1–3), ultimately fulfilled in the person and work of Jesus Christ. Throughout the Old Testament the descendants of Abram were used as channels of divine revelation. Prophets spoke orally to the people, and some of them wrote the Scriptures, including the opening books of the Bible written by Moses. In spite of increased knowledge of God and His moral standards, the human race became evil, and Israel, the immediate divine recipient of God's blessing, was also judged sinful and had to be dealt with in the captivities. The Old Testament, instead of being a revelation of improvement as envisioned in the theory of evolution, instead took man farther and farther from God with the result that the human race no longer had the longevity it did in creation and that many acts of violence and sin were performed.

After Jesus' birth in the New Testament with His subsequent life on earth, His rejection by His generation, His crucifixion and death for the sins of the whole world, and His glorious resurrection, a new chapter in the history of man begins. However, just as was true in the Old Testament, the human race, for the most part, rejected God and went on its wicked way.

In the present age God is calling out from both Jew and Gentile those who will believe in Christ and be saved. He is not attempting to judge the sins of the world, though sometimes there is divine judgment upon sin. Even with all the advanced revelation given in the writing of the New Testament and the presentation of Jesus Christ to the world, the moral history of the world has become more and more a record of departure from God.

The apostle Peter recorded in graphic tones how man departed from God and denied redemption by blood (2 Peter 2:1), and how religious leaders who were not saved would, like Balaam, lead people astray (2 Peter 2:15). This would continue even to the time of the second coming of Christ, when scoffers would reject the doctrine and refuse to believe that Christ is coming again to judge the world (2 Peter 3:3–4).

The apostle Paul in his last epistle in 2 Timothy 3:1–5 summarizes the awful extent of human sin, "But mark this: There will be terrible times in the last days. People will be lovers of themselves, lovers of money, boastful, proud, abusive, disobedient to their parents, ungrateful, unholy, without love, unforgiving, slanderous, without self-control, brutal, not lovers of the good, treacherous, rash, conceited, lovers of pleasure rather than lovers of God—having a form of godliness but denying its power."

The present age of grace will be followed by the Day of the Lord, an age in which God will deal directly with human sin in the time of trouble preceding the second coming of Christ, a time that continues throughout the millennial kingdom when His rule will be one of absolute authority. Though the millennial kingdom in many ways is a bright spot in the future history of the world, even in the millennial kingdom there is rebellion at the end when, in spite of all the divine revelation given to them in the Millennium, people will rebel against Christ and attempt to conquer Jerusalem by force.

In the sad destiny of the human race, there will be division of those who are saved and those who are lost, with the saved being in the presence of the Lord forever in the new heaven and the new earth and the new Jerusalem and the lost ultimately being cast into the lake of fire (Rev. 20:15). From God's viewpoint, out of the dark history of the human race will come those among angels and men who choose to worship God and who will share with them the joy and bliss of eternity in the presence of God in the new Jerusalem.

Questions

1. How do the Scriptures represent the creation of man?
2. What is the claim of the theory of evolution?
3. Why is organic evolution rejected by those who accept the Bible as the Word of God?
4. What solution does evolution have for the origin of life?

5. How does evolution fail to explain that in man which corresponds to the image of God?

6. How was Jesus Christ related to creation?

7. From what was the universe formed at God's command?

8. Why do scoffers have to begin with the concept of creation?

9. Define how man is divided into material and immaterial?

10. To what is "soul" referred to in man?

11. What does "spirit" refer to in man?

12. How are "soul" and "spirit" contrasted to "body"?

13. Why are these three terms sometimes used to represent the whole of man?

14. What immaterial aspects of man are mentioned in the Bible other than soul and spirit?

15. What is the contrast between the present sinful state of a person's body and his future body?

16. How has humankind attempted to solve the problem of sin in the world?

17. How does the Bible explain the entrance of sin into the human race?

18. In contrast to the world of philosophy, what does the Bible offer as a solution for the sin problem?

19. Why is it important to understand what the Bible teaches about sin?

20. How is physical death related to sin?

21. What curses did God pronounce upon Satan, woman, and man after Adam and Eve sinned?

22. How does the sin of Adam relate to us today?

23. How does God solve the sin problem for people today?

24. What is meant by imputation? And how is it used in the Bible?

25. What does it mean to be justified by faith?

26. How does history demonstrate that conscience is not enough to keep people from doing what is wrong?
27. What did God do in the time of Noah?
28. What principles of government were introduced after the flood?
29. What did the descendants of Noah demonstrate regarding sin at the Tower of Babel?
30. What did God promise Abram?
31. To what extent were the promises to Abram fulfilled?
32. How did the world as a whole react to the coming of Christ, His death, and His resurrection?
33. What is God's primary purpose in the present age?
34. Does the Bible predict that evil will get worse or that sin will be gradually overcome?
35. What age follows the present age of grace? And what does it include?

[5]

The Jew and the Gentile

Background of the Jew in the Old Testament

FOLLOWING THE FLOOD OF NOAH humankind was divided into three major racial divisions descending from the three sons of Noah—Shem, Ham, and Japheth. The entire human race descended from these three sons of Noah.

The sons of Japheth formed the largest group descending from Noah and include the peoples mentioned in Genesis 10:2–5 especially the peoples in Asia Minor, Greece, the Soviet Union, Cyprus, and Southeastern Europe. These people later spread to other parts of the world.

The sons of Ham, mentioned in Genesis 10:6–20, in general inhabited Asia, except for Northern Asia, and lived in Southern Europe and Northern Africa. Like others, they scattered throughout the world in subsequent history. They were the original inhabitants of the land that God later gave to Israel.

The sons of Shem, mentioned in Genesis 10:21–31, in general occupied the Middle East. Important to the Bible is the fact that the descendants of Shem included Abram and Israel and also Jesus Christ. Genesis 10 remains the most ancient document detailing the movement of the nations and the location of various peoples, and even the secular world has to turn to it for information.

As the history of the Old Testament unfolded after the flood, humankind continued to rebel against God, culminating in the judgment of the Tower of Babel (Gen. 11:1–9). In Genesis 12 a new divine purpose of God was revealed creating a new division, beginning with Abram. The rest of the book of Genesis, from chapter 11 to chapter 50, deals with Abram and his descendants. God promised that a special blessing would come to the whole earth through Abram's descendants. The line of this fulfillment went through Isaac, Abram's son, and then to Jacob, the son of Isaac, who was the father of the heads of the twelve tribes of Israel. Though Abram blessed the descendants of Ishmael and Isaac blessed Esau, the line of Isaac and Jacob alone inherited the promise of being a blessing to the whole world and the promises given to Jacob and his sons.

From the time of the emergence of Israel as a special people, God's plans for them in fulfillment of the Abrahamic Covenant are unfolded throughout the Old Testament. Under the rule of Kings Saul, David, and Solomon, Israel became a great nation, unexcelled for riches and glory. Following the death of Solomon, however, because of his intermarriage with many heathen wives, the kingdom was divided into two—the kingdom of Israel, including the ten tribes, and the kingdom of Judah, including the tribes of Judah and Benjamin. Beginning in the book of Esther and continuing with a few references in 2 Kings and 2 Chronicles, the two tribes of the kingdom of Judah were called Jews and carried off into captivity. This designation of "Jews" continued through the captivities, and in Ezra, Nehemiah, Esther, Jeremiah, and Daniel, and later in the New Testament. Though, strictly speaking, the title applied only to the tribe of Judah because it was the dominant tribe from which the kings came, eventually all twelve tribes began to be labeled as Jews. By contrast, all others became known as Gentiles, originally applied to some sons of Japheth (Gen. 10:5 KJV), but later to all those who were not descendants of Jacob (Neh. 5:8).

When the wise men came from the East seeking Jesus, they asked the question, "Where is the one who has been born king of the Jews?" (Matt. 2:2). The Magi were referring to the promise of a king over all twelve tribes of Israel. Though Israel is referred to in approximately 80 New Testament passages, the nation is designated "the Jews" in approximately 190 New Testament references.

The Jews as a Separate People

The study of the Jew in the Old Testament clearly reveals that God has a special purpose for this people. Paul described this special place in these words, "Theirs is the adoption as sons; theirs the divine glory, the covenants, the receiving of the law, the temple worship and the promises. Theirs are the patriarchs, and from them is traced the human ancestry of Christ, who is God over all, forever praised! Amen" (Rom. 9:4–5).

As the summary in Romans 9 indicates, the Jews were a special people who were designed by God to be the channel of divine revelation to the world. From them would come the prophets, the writers of the Old Testament, and most of the writers of the New Testament. From them would come the twelve apostles and, supremely, Jesus Christ. The Jews were given the Law of Moses, which was not extended beyond Israel. To them were given the special rules for worship in the tabernacle and in the temple; and to them were given special promises that were not extended to the entire human race. Though Israel did not choose God, God chose them; and with extraordinary patience and tenacity, He fulfills His promises to Israel even in times of apostasy and departure from God. It is in keeping with this purpose of God that Israel had such a prominent place throughout the Old Testament, and the course of human history is developed in the Old Testament period as it revolves around Israel and the Holy Land. God's dealing with them both in judgment and in mercy provided a divine revelation of the nature of God, His righteousness, His love, His grace, and His infinite wisdom. The major movements of the nation constitute the important divisions of the Old Testament. In the time of Jacob and Joseph the children of Israel went down to Egypt a family of seventy, and there, in several hundred years, they became a great nation of perhaps two to three million.

After the Jews fell into ill favor with Pharaoh and they became slaves, God raised up Moses to lead them from Egypt to the Promised Land. After Moses' death Joshua brought the children of Israel into the land that they possessed.

After Israel went through the apostasies recorded in the book of Judges, they became a great nation, beginning with Samuel the prophet and then Kings Saul, David, and Solomon. After Solomon's death, however, their continued sinfulness against God not only resulted in the division of the two kingdoms—the ten tribes, the kingdom of Israel, and the two tribes, the kingdom of Judah—but God caused them to be taken out of the land. The ten tribes were carried off by Assyria in 722 B.C. (1 Chron. 5:25–26), and the remaining two tribes, the kingdom of Judah, were conquered by Babylon in 605 B.C. Judah was subsequently carried off to Babylon, and Jerusalem, along with its beautiful temple, was plundered and destroyed in 586 B.C. (2 Chron. 36:17–20).

In 538 B.C. under Ezra, fifty thousand came back to try to reestablish Israel in the land (Ezra 1:1–2:70). After many years of struggle Nehemiah arrived on the scene in 445 B.C. and encouraged them to rebuild the wall and rebuild the city (Neh. 1:1–6:16; 11:1–2). When Christ was born, Jerusalem was once again a thriving city.

The subsequent rejection of Christ ultimately resulted in the dispersion of the children of Israel all over the world, beginning in A.D. 70 when Jerusalem was conquered and burned by the Romans.

In the twentieth century the children of Israel have begun their return to their ancient land, signaling what may well be the beginning of the final regathering of Israel prophesied in Scripture. Almost four million Jews now live within the bounds of the land of Israel and are in their place to fulfill their prophetic destiny.

The Gentiles as a Separate People

While the Old Testament gives major attention to the people of Israel and portrays their special place in the plan of God, the revelation of God's special purpose for the Gentiles also is unfolded in the Old Testament.

The large place that the Gentiles would play in subsequent history has as its background the ethnological table of the descendants of Noah found in Genesis 10. No other ancient document gives the material of the origin of the various races as does this chapter. From a biblical standpoint it is important because it provides a background for history and prophecy as they relate to all other peoples who are not descendants of Jacob.

The Egyptian Empire

The major role of the Gentiles is traced first to the nation of Egypt, which at one time was the most powerful nation in the world. Abram, according to Genesis 12:10, went down to Egypt, where he attempted to gain favor by saying that Sarai was his sister, not his wife (Gen. 12:10–13). Actually, she was his half-sister. This almost proved disastrous as Pharaoh took Sarai into the palace to become his wife (Gen. 12:14–16). Though Sarai was more than sixty-five years of age, she was declared to be a beautiful and desirable woman. When Abram's deceit was discovered, he left Egypt (Gen. 12:17–20), but not without some of the riches that he had accumulated in the short time there. Unfortunately, he also took with him a slave girl, Hagar, who later became the mother of Ishmael (Gen. 16:1–15).

When Isaac later wanted to go down into Egypt, God appeared to him and told him to stay in the land and he would inherit the promises that God gave to Abram (Gen. 26:1–6).

The most important chapter in Israel's history occurred in the time of Jacob and Joseph when the children of Israel went down to Egypt to escape the famine (Gen. 46:1–7). Joseph, because he had interpreted Pharaoh's dream concerning the coming famine (Gen. 41:1–43), was able to care for his people (Gen. 46:28–47:12), and in the several hundred years that they dwelt in Egypt they became a nation of two to three million. Subsequently, under Moses they left Egypt (Ex. 12:31–51), and under Joshua they conquered most of the Promised Land

(Josh. 21:43–45), though some sections remained unconquered (Judges 1:21, 27–28).

The Assyrian Empire

As the years passed, Assyria rose in power and supplanted Egypt as the most dominant nation in the Middle East. The Assyrian armies were those who carried off the ten tribes into captivity in 722 B.C. (1 Chron. 5:25–26).

Assyria, however, was defeated in 612 B.C., and its capital city, Nineveh, was burned. The Assyrian empire was then succeeded by the empire of Babylon.

The Empires Revealed to Daniel: Babylon, Medo-Persia, Greece, and Rome

The Babylonians played an important part in the history of Israel because they were responsible for the conquering of Jerusalem in 605 B.C. and the subsequent captivity of Judah.

Most significant in the revelation of God's purposes for the Gentiles was the truth revealed through Daniel that beginning with Babylon there would be four great world empires prior to the kingdom that would come from heaven. In Daniel 2 this was revealed to Nebuchadnezzar, the king of Babylon, in a gigantic image that had a head of gold, the upper part of the body of silver, the lower part of the body of bronze, the legs of iron, and the feet of iron and pottery. As Daniel interpreted this dream for the king (Dan. 2), the various elements of the image revealed the four empires—the head of gold being Babylon, the upper part of the body of silver being that of the Medes and the Persians, the lower part of the body of bronze referring to the kingdom of

Greece or the conquest of Alexander the Great, and the legs of iron and the feet of iron and pottery representing the empire of Rome. The first three empires are named in the book of Daniel (2:36–38; 5:30; 8:20–21). The fourth empire most naturally represents Rome, which succeeded the Grecian Empire.

In Daniel 7 the prophecies of the future of the Gentiles were further revealed in the form of four beasts. In Daniel 7 the lion represents Babylon, the bear represents Medo-Persia, the leopard represents Alexander, king of Greece, and his conquests, and the beast with great iron teeth represents the empire of Rome. Greece is named in Daniel 8:21 and represented as the goat with one prominent horn, referring to Alexander, and Medo-Persia is pictured as a ram with two horns (Dan. 8:2–4, 20). The fourth beast represents Rome.

The Future Revival of the Roman Empire

Most significant are the details furnished concerning the Roman Empire. Though most of the prophecy concerning Rome has now been fulfilled in history, the final stage is represented by a beast having ten horns, according to Daniel 7:7. A little horn (7:8) arises, however, which uproots three of the ten horns, and this is interpreted as a ruler who eventually will gain control of the Roman Empire. As this ten-horned stage has never occurred in history, it seems that the vision leaps to the present age without taking into consideration the time between the first and second coming of Christ and centers on the final form of world government in the end time preceding the second coming of Christ.

The ten-horn stage of the beast represents the revived Roman Empire composed of ten kingdoms in and around the Mediterranean Sea. The "little horn" of Daniel 7:8 represents its ruler who eventually becomes a world ruler. As stated in Daniel 7:23, "It will be different from all the other kingdoms and will devour the whole earth, trampling it down and crushing it." The truth represented in Daniel's prophetic vision is given further detail in the book of Revelation, especially in Revelation 13.

The Prophetic Program for Jews and Gentiles Culminates in the Second Coming

The program for Israel as well as for the Gentiles in Daniel's prophecies culminates in the second coming of Christ, when Gentile dominion will be destroyed and Israel will be restored to her ancient land.

God's special purposes for Israel included that through them would come the Messiah and the Savior in the person of the Lord Jesus Christ in His first coming, and that through them would come divine revelation to the world in the form of prophetic utterance and biblical writings. Through Israel God would reveal Himself as He had never revealed Himself before.

In the history of the Gentiles and in their ultimate prophetic future, God demonstrates His sovereignty over the world, and the Gentiles form the special vehicle that shows the power and wisdom of God that ultimately will bring every race and every people into subjection to Himself. Gentile history in the Old Testament as well as the prophecy of its future, accordingly, forms the graphic background for what God has accomplished in and through Israel. These lines of truth will continue and ultimately be fulfilled at the Second Coming and in the millennial kingdom.

Questions

1. What were the names of Noah's three children?
2. What is their importance to the history of the race?
3. From what son of Noah did Christ and the people of Israel descend?
4. What form did rebellion against God take among the descendants of Noah?
5. What new divine purpose of God is revealed in Genesis 12?
6. What is the significance of the fact that God devotes from Genesis 11 to Genesis 50 to the history of Abraham, Isaac, and Jacob?
7. What was the line of fulfillment of the promise to Abram's seed?
8. What happened to Israel under Kings Saul, David, and Solomon?
9. Why did the kingdom after Solomon divide into two kingdoms?
10. Trace the designation "Jews" to the people of Israel.
11. When the Magi came from the East seeking Jesus, what did they have in mind in reference to the promise of a king?
12. What are some of the outstanding features that God bestowed on Israel as a separate people according to Romans 9?
13. To what extent did God use Israel as a channel of divine revelation? What did God reveal in His dealings with Israel through the centuries?
14. What caused the children of Israel to go down into Egypt?
15. How did they travel from Egypt to the Promised Land?

16. What was the moral situation in Israel prior to Samuel the prophet?
17. What did God do to the ten tribes who had rebelled against Him?
18. What did He do to the two remaining tribes?
19. When did the people of Israel go back to their land? Describe the struggles of the pilgrims who returned to Jerusalem and the ultimate outcome.
20. What happened to Israel in A.D. 70 and in the following years?
21. Trace the relationship of Egypt to the children of Israel?
22. What was Abram's experience in Egypt?
23. State briefly Assyria's rise to power and subsequent decline.
24. What four empires were revealed prophetically to Daniel?
25. What part did the Babylonians play in the history of Israel?
26. In regard to the image in Nebuchadnezzar's vision, describe the identification of the head of gold, the upper part of the body of silver, the lower part of the body of bronze, the legs of iron, and the feet of iron and pottery.
27. What will succeed the fourth empire?
28. In Daniel's vision of the four beasts in Daniel 7, how do you identify the four beasts?
29. How much of this has been fulfilled?
30. In regard to the unfulfilled prophecies concerning Rome, what may we expect to emerge in the end time?
31. When will the period of Gentile power finally end?
32. What, in general, does God demonstrate in His handling of the Gentile world?

[6]

Jesus Christ:
Messiah and Savior

Jesus Christ as God

THE MOST IMPORTANT EVENT recorded in Scripture is the coming of Jesus Christ as the Son of God and as the Savior of those who trust Him. The most important event in the life of a Christian is when he comes to faith in Jesus Christ as his Savior. In the introduction to the gospel of John, Jesus is given the title of "the Word," meaning that He is the precise expression of who God is. Hebrews 1:2–3 expresses it this way:

> In these last days he has spoken to us by his Son, whom he appointed heir of all things, and through whom he made the universe. The Son is the radiance of God's glory and the exact representation of his being, sustaining all things by his powerful word. After he had provided purification for sins, he sat down at the right hand of the Majesty in heaven.

Jesus Christ as Creator

John's gospel goes on to speak of Christ as the Creator, "Through him all things were made; without him nothing was made that has been made" (John 1:3). John continues to refer to Christ not only as the Creator but one who has life in Himself and whose life constitutes a divine revelation of the light of men, "In him was life, and that life was the light of men" (John 1:4). When a believer in Christ is saved, he receives eternal life and at the same time he sees the light, and God's truth becomes understandable to him.

Jesus Christ Rejected in His First Coming

As John unfolds the place of Jesus Christ and His purpose in coming into the world, he is concerned that the world has not received Him, especially when receiving Him is so important. John writes, "He was in the world, and though the world was made through him, the world did not recognize him. He came to that which was his own, but his own did not receive him. Yet to all who received him, to those who believed in his name, he gave the right to become children of God—children born not of natural descent, nor of human decision or a husband's will, but born of God. The Word became flesh and made his dwelling among us. We have seen his glory, the glory of the One and Only, who came from the Father, full of grace and truth" (John 1:10–14).

In this tremendous statement John points out how Jesus came to His own world, which He had created, but His own people did not receive Him; on the other hand, there were those who did receive Him, and they had the right to become children of God. He points out how their new birth is not of human design or will, but that they are born of God. Then he summarizes the fact that the "Word," referring to Jesus Christ, "became flesh," that is, He became incarnate and "made his dwelling among us," meaning that He lived on earth. John speaks of the fact that he had seen the glory of Christ even though the glory was normally veiled. He was referring to the Transfiguration (Matt. 17:1–8; Mark 9:2–13; Luke 9:28–36). Though His full glory was not seen by most people, nevertheless, it is true that Jesus Christ came from the Father and that His whole purpose was full of grace and truth, that is, He was the supreme manifestation, both in His ministry in truth and as the One who died on the cross for our sins. He is "full of grace and truth" for the world to behold (John 1:14).

Purpose to Provide Salvation

Jesus Christ's main purpose in coming to the world, however, was to provide salvation for those who put their trust in Him. Jesus expressed this in Luke 19:10, "For the Son of Man came to seek and to save what was lost."

In His public ministry Jesus spoke of many truths, and His teachings were so comprehensive that a systematic theology could be written based on what He said and taught. However, this was a background to His dying on the cross for our sins. In this supreme act of dying, He fulfilled His main purpose in becoming incarnate, of being "the Lamb of God, who takes away the sin of the world" (John 1:29).

In His resurrection from the dead, He also manifested His deity and His power to fulfill His own word in that He had power to lay down His life and He had power to take it up again (John 10:18). In connection with the death of Christ, three important theological terms are used to express what Christ did when He died on the cross for our sins: redemption, propitiation, and reconciliation.

Redemption: Purchase of Salvation

The doctrine of redemption declares that Christ bought us and paid the price for our deliverance from sin. The concept of redemption comes from the Greek word *agorazo* which means to go into the marketplace to buy. Six times in the Bible Christians are said to be "bought," or "redeemed," in regard to the death of Christ (1 Cor. 6:20; 7:23; 2 Peter 2:1; Rev. 5:9; 14:3–4). In 1 Corinthians 6:19–20 it states, "You are not your own; you were bought at a price. Therefore honor God with your body." The idea of a slave being bought is mentioned in 1 Corinthians 7:23, "You were bought at a price; do not become slaves of men."

In 2 Peter 2:1 a very important Scripture is recorded, "But there were also false prophets among the people, just as there will be false teachers among you. They will secretly introduce destructive heresies, even denying the sovereign Lord who bought them—bringing swift destruction upon themselves." This passage is quite important because it indicates that redemption does not only extend to those who are saved but also is God's provision for those who are lost. In this passage in 2 Peter even the false teachers who were contradicting the gospel are said to have been "bought" (Gr. *agorazo*), but they did not avail themselves of salvation and continue to be lost. This is part of the important evidence in Scripture that when Christ died He did not die just for the elect, as some have taught, but He died for the whole world, making the world saveable, even if it is also true that only the elect are saved.

In Revelation 5:8–9 the four living creatures and the twenty-four elders sing a new song of redemption:

When he had taken [the scroll], the four living creatures and the twenty-four elders fell down before the Lamb. Each one had a harp and they were holding golden bowls full of incense, which are the prayers of the saints. And they sang a new song: "You are worthy to take the scroll and to open its seals, because you were slain, and with your blood you purchased men for God from every tribe and language and people and nation."

This passage teaches that Christ had a right to save those who were desperately lost because He had died for them and paid the price for their sins. In Revelation 14:3 the 144,000 were those "who had been redeemed from the earth."

Another Greek verb used to express the intensive character of the redemption in Christ is the Greek word *exagorazo*. This is found four times in the New Testament (Gal. 3:13; 4:5; Eph. 5:16; Col. 4:5). In Galatians 3:13 we are said to be redeemed and delivered from the law which condemned us. The same thought is given in Galatians 4:5. The point is that we were not only "bought" by the redemption in Christ but we were taken out of the marketplace, that is, we were bought out of the market, and given security and set free as those who were formerly slaves. Colossians 4:5 and Ephesians 5:16 refer to redeeming the time or making the most of time in regard to the Lord's return.

Another expression is used to indicate redemption, and this is the Greek word *peripoieo*, which occurs three times in the New Testament (Luke 17:33; Acts 20:28; 1 Tim. 3:13). This verb means "to be acquired," or "possessed," by the Lord. Accordingly, in Luke 17:33 it conveys the meaning of preserving life or acquiring it. In Acts 20:28 it carries the thought of being bought and possessed by the Lord, "Be shepherds of the church of God, which he bought with his own blood." In 1 Timothy 3:13 the thought again is that of being possessed by the Lord. Because we are redeemed and bought with the blood of Christ, we no longer belong to ourselves, but we belong to the Lord and are His possession.

Another important concept related to redemption is the idea of being freed from the burden and slavery of sin. This thought is brought out in numerous passages in the New Testament (Luke 21:28; Rom. 3:24; 8:23; 1 Cor. 1:30; Eph. 1:7, 14; 4:30; Col. 1:14; Heb. 9:15). Of these, Romans 3:24 is a good illustration of this concept of being freed, "Justified freely by his grace through the redemption that came by Christ Jesus." Christ not only paid the price for our sins but freed us from the condemnation and slavery that is involved. This is the ultimate end of God's plan of redemption for those who put their trust in Christ.

The doctrine of redemption, therefore, speaks of (1) the purchase of our salvation by Christ, (2) being bought off the market and not subject to resale, (3) being a possession that is precious in the sight of the Lord, and (4) being set free, pardoned, and released from the burden of sin.

Propitiation: Satisfaction of God's Righteousness

The work of Christ in salvation has still another major aspect of what is called in the Bible "propitiation," "the sacrifice of atonement," or satisfying God's righteous demands or judgment upon a sinner. Illustrations of this can be found in Romans 3:25 and 1 John 2:2; 4:10. The idea of propitiation is that God as a righteous God must demand punishment for those who sin against Him. Christ in His death on the cross provided propitiation, atonement, or satisfaction of that claim, so that God is fully satisfied now in saving a person who does not deserve to be saved.

Following immediately the statement concerning redemption in Romans 3:24, verses 25 and 26 say, "God presented him as a sacrifice of atonement, through faith in his blood. He did this to demonstrate his justice, because in his forbearance he had left sins committed beforehand unpunished—he did it to demonstrate his justice at the present time, so as to be just and the one who justifies those who have faith in Jesus." The expression, "sacrifice of atonement," literally means a sacrifice of propitiation, or a sacrifice of satisfaction. In Christ's death on the cross, as this passage states, God is justified in having forgiven sins in the Old Testament even before the sacrifice was made. Christ's dying on the cross now demonstrates God's justice in forgiving sins of the past as well as sins to be committed in the future. Accordingly, God is both just Himself and able to justify, or declare righteous, those who have faith in Jesus.

The doctrine of propitiation is an important doctrine relating to our salvation. The New Testament frequently speaks of the wrath of God. In Christ's death on the cross He satisfied God's judicial wrath and His righteous indignation concerning sin and makes it possible for a righteous God to justly declare a sinner righteous.

Important results of this doctrine include the following: (1) God is declared justified or righteous in forgiving sin; (2) God is justified in bestowing righteousness on the believer; (3) God is justified in bestowing all grace on sinners because He is completely satisfied by the death of Christ. The central concept is that God has been satisfied concerning our sins and can freely give believers what they do not deserve. This is a great blessing to Christians who sense their inadequacy and imperfections and yet want to have close fellowship with the Lord.

Reconciliation of the Sinner to God

A third major truth of the death of Christ is in the doctrine of reconciliation, addressing the fact that a sinner is estranged from God and in Christ he is reconciled to God. Scholars have differed in their interpretation of reconciliation. A careful study, however, will support the view that reconciliation is toward the sinner just as propitiation is toward God and redemption is toward sin. The point is that man in his natural, sinful state is far below God and hopeless as far as fellowship with God is concerned. In the death of Christ reconciliation is provided, that is, a believer is so changed that he is made a son of God and has reckoned to his account the perfect righteousness of God in justification. This makes it possible for a Christian to be reconciled to God because he is lifted up to God's high standard.

This truth is discussed in several important passages (2 Cor. 5:17–21; Eph. 2:16; Col. 1:20–22). In 2 Corinthians 5:17–21 Paul articulates the doctrine of reconciliation:

> If anyone is in Christ, he is a new creation; the old has gone, the new has come! All this is from God, who reconciled us to himself through Christ and gave us the ministry of reconciliation: that God was reconciling the world to himself in Christ, not counting men's sins against them. And he has committed to us the message of reconciliation. We are therefore Christ's ambassadors, as though God were making his appeal through us. We implore you on Christ's behalf: Be reconciled to God. God made him who had no sin to be sin for us, so that in him we might become the righteousness of God.

The central thought of this passage is stated in verse 19, "that God was reconciling the world to himself in Christ, not counting men's sins against them." This is the marvelous message of God's salvation that He can take a sinner, however bad, and give him the transformed life as well as a transformed position of being in Christ, reconciled to God.

On the basis of this wonderful truth, Christians have committed to them the message of reconciliation, that is, they are to preach this word. As Paul expresses it, "We implore you on Christ's behalf: Be reconciled to God" (2 Cor. 5:20). The doctrine of reconciliation is summarized in 2 Corinthians 5:21: "God made him who had no sin to be sin for us, so that in him we might become the righteousness of God." This passage, like others in the New Testament, states the fact that Christ died for the world, that is, He died for all and provisionally provided for their reconciliation to God. The sad fact of the unsaved is that Christ died for them and that they are lost, not because God did not love them or provide for them, but because they did not avail themselves of what was offered to them by faith in Christ.

Earlier in 2 Corinthians 5:14–15 Paul says, "For Christ's love compels us, because we are convinced that one died for all, and therefore all died. And he died for all, that those who live should no longer live for themselves but for him who died for them and was raised again." The three mentions of the word "all" make clear that Christ died for the entire world when He died. By contrast, however, those who put their faith in Christ are a portion of the world referred to as "those who live." The benefit of the death of Christ is limited to those who put their trust in Christ and become saved.

The doctrine of reconciliation makes possible all the other works of God for those who are in Christ, including their regeneration, their baptism into the body of Christ, the indwelling of the Holy Spirit, their justification, their new position in Christ, and their ultimate sanctification. Only a God of infinite grace and infinite wisdom could have devised such a wonderful plan of salvation for those who put their trust in Christ.

Questions

1. Why is the coming of Christ so important?
2. Why is the most important event in the life of a Christian when he comes to faith in Jesus Christ as his Savior?
3. How is the revelation of Jesus Christ, mentioned in Hebrews 1:2–3, summarized?
4. To what extent is Jesus Christ the Creator according to John?
5. When does a believer receive the life that is in Christ?
6. When does a believer receive Christ as the light of men?
7. How does John record the rejection of Jesus by his generation?
8. When a person receives Christ, what does he have a right to become?
9. How is the new birth contrasted to natural birth?
10. When did the apostle John see Christ in His glory?
11. How is the truth expressed relative to the main purpose of Christ in coming into the world?
12. What was accomplished by Christ in dying on the cross?
13. What was accomplished by His resurrection from the dead?
14. What is the meaning of redemption? Did Christ die for everyone? Does this mean that everyone is saved?

15. How is redemption related to security of the believer and his salvation?
16. To what extent is the believer freed from the burden and slavery of sin?
17. What is the meaning of propitiation?
18. What completely satisfies divine justice in regard to the sinner?
19. How does propitiation relate to the fact that God is freely able to save and to bestow grace upon sinners?
20. What is meant by a sinner being reconciled to God?
21. What is our message of reconciliation?
22. How does regeneration, baptism of the Spirit, indwelling of the Holy Spirit, justification, the Christian's new position, and his ultimate sanctification relate to reconciliation?

[7]

What Must I Do to Be Saved?

IF GOD HAS PROVIDED a wonderful salvation through Christ as revealed in the Bible, how can anyone be sure that he has received Christ and is the beneficiary of this marvelous grace of God?

The question of what one must do to be saved was asked long ago by the Philippian jailor in Acts 16:30. Paul and Silas had been beaten and thrown into prison in Philippi, with their feet fastened in the stocks. In this painful condition they could not sleep, so they sang praises to God. Scripture records that at midnight, as they were praying, there was an earthquake that broke them loose from their bonds and opened the prison doors. The jailor, rushing out and seeing the doors opened, assumed that the prisoners had fled. Because the law demanded that a jailor who lost prisoners should be put to death, he was about to commit suicide when Paul called out to him to do himself no harm because they were still all there. In response to this information, Scripture records that the jailor, after calling for some lights, fell down before Paul, trembling and

pleading, "Sirs, what must I do to be saved?" (Acts 16:30).
Paul and Silas both immediately responded as recorded in
Acts 16:31, "Believe in the Lord Jesus, and you will be
saved—you and your household." As a result of the jailor's
conversion, his entire house also believed and was saved,
and he took Paul out of the jail, washed his wounds and
had fellowship with him. But how can one living today be
assured that he is saved?

In discussing God's wonderful plan of salvation in
Ephesians 2:8–10, the apostle Paul sums it up in three
verses, "For it is by grace you have been saved, through
faith—and this not from yourselves, it is the gift of
God—not by works, so that no one can boast. For we are
God's workmanship, created in Christ Jesus to do good
works, which God prepared in advance for us to do."

By Grace

The most important aspect of salvation is mentioned
in the first part of Ephesians 2:8 where it states that we are
saved "by grace." The word *grace* has various meanings,
but as it relates to salvation it speaks of kindness bestowed
on one who does not deserve it. In other words, grace
pours favor on those who do not deserve favor. In grace,
the question is not whether or not a person deserves favor
or blessing, but only whether he has been judged to qualify
for such favor.

An examination of scriptural texts brings out how
prominent this is in our Christian faith. In Romans 3:24 Paul
says that Christians "are justified freely by his grace through
the redemption that came by Christ Jesus." In other words,
because Christ paid the price and provided redemption, it is
now possible for a Christian to receive grace, or favor, that
he does not deserve. In Ephesians 1:7–8 the apostle speaks

of the riches of grace in Christ when he says, "In him we have redemption through his blood, the forgiveness of sins, in accordance with the riches of God's grace that he lavished upon us with all wisdom and understanding." In every instance where grace is mentioned, it is entirely due to God's favor, not human works.

Through Faith

According to Ephesians 2:8, grace is received by those who exercise faith in Jesus Christ. This introduces, however, a very practical question as to what is meant by faith. It is rather obvious for any careful observer of the church today that there are many who have made some outward profession of faith in Christ who never have been born again and show no evidence that they are saved. How then can one know whether he has put his faith in Christ or not? According to James 2:19, "Even the devils believe that—and shudder." From these passages it is clear that there is saving faith and faith that does not save.

Convicting Work of the Holy Spirit

True faith in Christ is preceded by the work of the Spirit as Jesus Himself described in John 16:7–11:

But I tell you the truth: It is for your good that I am going away. Unless I go away, the Counselor will not come to you; but if I go, I will send him to you. When he comes, he will convict the world of guilt in regard to sin and righteousness and judgment: in regard to sin, because men do not believe in me; in regard to righteousness, because I am going to the Father, where you can see me no longer; and in regard to judgment, because the prince of this world now stands condemned.

Before a person can intelligently believe in Christ, he has to be aware of the guilt of his sin. He also must face the fact that God is righteous and that He judges sin. This is further defined in verse 9, "in regard to sin, because men do not believe in me." An unsaved person needs to realize that while he is a sinner, as all men are sinners, this constitutes only a part of his condemnation before God. The one sin that prevents him from entering into grace and favor with God is the sin of unbelief. Accordingly, he must realize that salvation is by faith alone. He also needs instruction on the matter of righteousness. Scriptures reveal various kinds of righteousness, for instance, the false righteousness of human works. Scripture makes clear that any human works that we offer, even if they are good, do not qualify us for salvation. Isaiah 64:6 says, "All of us have become like one who is unclean, and all our righteous acts are like filthy rags." What the sinner needs to learn is that nothing short of the righteousness of God will allow him to be saved.

Judgment is also defined as referring to the fact that sin was judged when Christ died on the cross, and Satan was condemned and now awaits the execution of God's judgment. Obviously, many who are saved do not completely understand this doctrine, but, nevertheless, under compulsion of the Holy Spirit, turn to Christ in faith in order to be saved. The three aspects of the Spirit's convicting the unsaved are (1) that a person seeking salvation must understand the nature of sin in contrast to the righteousness of God, (2) that God provides a righteousness which is by faith and is not earned or deserved, and (3) that God has judged sin in Christ on the cross, including the condemnation of Satan. As we enter into salvation through faith in Christ, Christ becomes our sin-bearer. As John the

Baptist expressed it, Jesus Christ is the "Lamb of God, who takes away the sin of the world!" (John 1:29).

Salvation is from the Lord

When one considers all the facts relating to salvation and the preparatory work of the Spirit before one can be saved, it becomes obvious that simply assenting to the fact of the gospel and believing mentally that Jesus Christ died for the sins of the world does not result in salvation and is not really what can be called "saving faith."

In the nature of faith, it is also important to realize that it must come from the whole man, that is, from his intellect, sensibility, and will. There has to be some mental understanding of what the gospel is in order to be saved, and the sinner coming to Christ should enter into the fact that it requires more than assent—it requires an act of the whole person. This may involve not only the mind but the feelings, or sensibility, and, most of all, it involves the will, for faith is actually a step authorized by our will. The English word *belief* comes somewhat short of what is anticipated in the Bible, which is more accurately expressed as *trust*, or committing oneself to faith in Christ.

This is illustrated by the use of an elevator. A person may believe that the elevator is in good working order and would take him to the top floor of the building if he chose to get on board; but as long as he is outside the elevator, his belief that the elevator would take him to the top floor does not do him any good. Faith would mean that he stepped in the elevator and put his weight into it and committed himself to its mechanical perfections. Likewise, there is more than mere assent in the matter of believing in Christ. Saving faith involves the work of the Spirit as well as the whole person—intellect, sensibility, and will.

Because a person is dead spiritually, it also requires a work of God to draw him to Christ. Christ expressed it this way: "No one can come to me unless the Father has enabled him" (John 6:65).

Accordingly, in Scripture faith in Christ is an act of the whole person. It involves the work of the Spirit in the conviction of sin and righteousness and judgment, and it involves God's providing special enablement to one who is spiritually dead to believe in Christ. This is what the Bible defines as "saving faith."

While in our limitations it is not possible to understand completely what happens when a person trusts in Christ, the Scriptures are clear that it requires not only our action, but an act of God to bring it to consummation. Yet, the Scriptures make it plain that it is not faith plus works but faith that produces works that results in the salvation of an individual. The Father must draw the seeking sinner to Him for Jesus said, "No one can come to me unless the Father who sent me draws him, and I will raise him up at the last day" (John 6:44). Accordingly, on the divine side there must be an activity of God in drawing the sinner to Himself; there must be the convicting work of the Spirit; and then the individual, empowered by God, must respond by an act of his will to put his trust in Christ as his Savior.

In Ephesians 2:8 Paul goes on to say, "This [is] not from yourselves, it is the gift of God." Theologians have argued about what the word "this" refers to, and some have taken the position that "this" refers to faith. In other words, God must give faith or a person will not believe. But the Bible is not saying that faith is the gift of God in the sense of God doing the believing, but that the whole plan of salvation is the gift of God. Though some have tried to make "this" refer to faith, the word "this" is in the neuter gender, and faith is in the feminine gender. If "this" referred to faith, it would also have to be feminine. God does not believe for us. Instead, God enables a person who is spiritually dead to believe. The result is that faith is an act of the will of people made possible by the work of God.

Therefore, the whole work of salvation—by grace through faith and all the other elements that enter into salvation—is a work of God. Jonah 2:9 states, "Salvation comes from the LORD." A similar thought is provided in Revelation 7:10 where the multitude of the saved in heaven cry out with the song, "Salvation belongs to our God, who sits on the throne, and to the Lamb."

Not by Works

In an effort to distinguish true faith from mere assent, some have found it necessary to add requirements to the single requirement of faith for salvation. In keeping with this goal, they have required a person who wants to be saved to accept the lordship of Christ and to promise to serve the Lord from then on. This has been made a prerequisite to faith. This view is contradicted in Scripture where works follow faith but do not precede it. That is why in Ephesians 2:9 the apostle Paul makes it very explicit when he says, "Not by works so that no one can boast." He goes on to say that we have to be renewed to do good works, "for we are God's workmanship, created in Christ Jesus to do good works, which God prepared in advance for us to do" (Eph. 2:10).

If it is difficult for Christians always to be fully yielded to the Lord and acknowledge Christ as the Master and Lord of our lives, how much more difficult and impossible is it for a person who is unsaved to take such a step before he is born again and before he is saved. The scriptural approach is rather to recognize that there is superficial faith—mere assent—which does not bring salvation, and even Satan recognizes the facts about Jesus Christ and believes them but is not saved. On the other hand, where salvation is dealt with in Scripture, faith is the sole requirement for salvation, but it is faith in which all the elements combine, that is, it is an act of the human will and the human mind and the human capacity for emotion. It also includes a work of the Father who draws the sinner to Himself, and a work of the Holy Spirit in bringing conviction of sin, and righteousness, and judgment. In other words, it is faith alone, but it is the kind of faith that saves. It is real faith and real commitment to Jesus Christ as Savior.

Once a person is saved and has recognized the deity of Christ, then, as his Christian life unfolds, he is confronted with the task of living as a Christian ought to live. This, of course, is exactly what the Bible indicates. As stated in Ephesians 2:8–10, salvation is not by works, but salvation produces works; and when the individual is a new creature in Christ, he then is able to do things that are well pleasing to God in time and eternity. Therefore, one should not minimize the necessity for real faith as compared to mere mental assent; salvation requires real faith. Nor should one require works as a condition for salvation or as a requirement for faith before faith is exercised. Rather, once a person is saved, or born again, he then has the capacity to serve the Lord and, as stated in Romans 12:1–2, he is urged to present his body as a living sacrifice to fulfill the perfect will of God.

Questions

1. Describe how the jailor became saved.
2. What did Paul tell the jailor to do?

3. What did Paul mean when he said that we are saved by grace in Ephesians 2?

4. If salvation were by works, what works would a person have to do to be saved?

5. Is salvation a work of God for us or a work that we do for God?

6. What does the word *grace* mean in relation to salvation?

7. How does Romans 3:24 define the nature of grace?

8. What does Paul refer to as "the riches of God's grace" in Ephesians 1:7–8?

9. Why is salvation, according to Ephesians 2:8, through faith?

10. Are there some who believe yet are not saved?

11. How can we tell whether we have true faith in Christ?

12. How does the convicting work of the Holy Spirit relate to faith?

13. What does the Spirit of God reveal to an individual in convicting him?

14. What was the special message regarding grace that was the special object of the Holy Spirit's revelation?

15. What did the Spirit of God reveal concerning righteousness?

16. What does Isaiah 64:6 teach us regarding works as a basis for salvation?

17. What happened to Satan when Christ died on the cross?

18. Summarize the three aspects of the Spirit's convicting work in relation to a person seeking salvation.

19. Is mental assent to the facts about Jesus Christ the same as saving faith?

20. How does the human mind, sensibility or feeling, and will enter into the matter of salvation?

21. How does an elevator illustrate faith?
22. What is meant by the statement that "faith in Christ is an act of the whole person"?
23. Where is the teaching that a person is saved by faith plus works contradicted by the Scripture?
24. What is the "gift of God" in Ephesians 2:8?
25. Why does Paul go out of his way to say that salvation is "not by works" in Ephesians 2:9?
26. According to Romans 12:1–2, when a person is saved, what should he do regarding his body?

[8]

God's Provision of a Complete Salvation

THE BIBLE NOT ONLY gives a full revelation of Jesus Christ as the Savior but also reveals in detail what happens the moment a person is saved. It becomes very obvious as one studies this in the Bible that salvation is something that God does for us, not something we do for God.

The New Birth

When a person believes in Jesus Christ as his Savior, one of the dramatic results is that he is born again, or regenerated. Many Scriptures are related to this doctrine (John 1:13; 3:3–7; 5:21; Rom. 6:13; 2 Cor. 5:17; Eph. 2:5, 10; 4:24; Titus 3:5; James 1:18; 1 Peter 2:9). As stated in John 1:13, one is not born again by any human effort but is "born of God." In His conversation with Nicodemus in John 3:3, Jesus declared, "I tell you the truth, no one can see the kingdom of God unless he is born again."

Nicodemus had trouble understanding how a person could be born again. Christ pointed out to him that one who puts his trust in Christ receives eternal life, "Just as

Moses lifted up the snake in the desert, so the Son of Man must be lifted up, that everyone who believes in him may have eternal life" (John 3:14–15). Jesus illustrated faith by referring to the time when Israel was bitten by poisonous snakes (Num. 21:6–7). God instructed Moses to make a bronze snake and put it on a pole. The Scriptures record, "So Moses made a bronze snake and put it up on a pole. Then when anyone was bitten by a snake and looked at the bronze snake, he lived" (Num. 21:8–9). The provision of the bronze snake was for everyone who was bitten by the serpent, but they had to look at the bronze snake to live. In like manner, Christ died for all, but it is necessary for an individual to look to Christ in faith before he is born again.

The fact of regeneration is stated in the well-known verse, John 3:16, "For God so loved the world that he gave his one and only Son, that whoever believes in him shall not perish but have eternal life." Many other passages reveal the same truth that when one trusts in Christ he is born again. The new birth is one of several illustrations that refer to a Christian's receiving life. The Scriptures also speak of spiritual resurrection as stated in Romans 6:13, "Do not offer the parts of your body to sin, as instruments of wickedness, but rather offer yourselves to God, as those who have been brought from death to life; and offer the parts of your body to him as instruments of righteousness." Here, salvation represents new life as being similar to spiritual resurrection.

Likewise, Scripture sometimes speaks of the new birth as a new creation as in 2 Corinthians 5:17 where Paul says, "If anyone is in Christ, he is a new creation; the old has gone, the new has come!"

When an individual is born again he has received a new nature like the human nature in Christ. Just as a child born by natural birth receives the nature of his parents, so in the new birth a Christian receives that which corresponds to God's nature making possible fellowship with God and many other aspects of Christian experience. Because the new birth by its nature cannot be reversed any more than natural birth can be reversed, it points to the fact that a Christian who is saved by God can have assurance of salvation for time and for eternity. Having received a new nature, however, a believer retains his old nature as well.

The Baptism of the Holy Spirit

Though any observer of Christianity recognizes that water baptism is a part of the Christian ordinances that characterize the Christian church, there is often little understanding of what spiritual baptism is. Actually, water baptism is the symbol of what is accomplished by the baptism of the Holy Spirit. In the New Testament there are eleven references to spiritual baptism (Matt. 3:11; Mark 1:8; Luke 3:16; John 1:33; Acts 1:5; 11:16; Rom. 6:1–4; 1 Cor. 12:13; Gal. 3:27; Eph. 4:5; Col. 2:12). In the gospels there is prophetic mention of the baptism of the Holy Spirit, and the prophecy of Acts 1:5 was fulfilled at Pentecost. After Pentecost the baptism of the Spirit is considered as a historic fact. The work of the Holy Spirit in baptizing provided (1) a new union with Christ, (2) a new position in Christ, and (3) a new association with Christ and a Christian's fellow believers.

There has been much confusion about the baptism of the Spirit because some consider it the same as the indwelling and filling of the Spirit, and others consider it the same as the new birth. The indwelling of the Spirit is His presence in the believer. The filling of the Spirit occurs when a believer yields himself to the Spirit. On the day of Pentecost all three took place at the same time, but the baptism of the Spirit, though it is received by everyone who is born again in the present age, is a distinct concept as is the filling and the indwelling of the Holy Spirit.

The main text on the baptism of the Spirit is 1 Corinthians 12:13, which states, "For we were all baptized by one Spirit into one body—whether Jews or Greeks, slave or free—and we were all given the one Spirit to drink." As stated here and illustrated in other instances, the baptism of the Spirit causes a new union *with Christ* and also is the work of the Holy Spirit in placing the believer *in Christ*. It is a matter of our position in relation to Christ. Another result is a new relationship to fellow believers who are also in Christ. The baptism of the Spirit is that work of God which forms the church as the body of Christ. It is, accordingly, very important in our understanding of what happens at the time of salvation, even though in itself it is not an experience.

Christians are never urged to be baptized by the Spirit because it is automatic at the time of the new birth. Every Christian is baptized by the Holy Spirit as stated in 1 Corinthians 12:13. Also, in Ephesians 4:5 Paul stresses "one Lord, one faith, one baptism."

The baptism of the Spirit introduces the important doctrine of the church as the body of Christ in contrast to the church as an organization. Many Scriptures relate to the church as the body of Christ (Acts 2:47; 1 Cor. 6:15; 12:12–14; Eph. 2:16; 4:4–5, 16; 5:30–32; Col. 1:24; 2:19). In the figure of the church as the body of Christ, the human body is a figure that represents the church, and Christ is revealed as the head of the body who directs the church (1 Cor. 11:3; Eph. 1:22–23; 5:23–24; Col. 1:18). Just as the human body has many parts with various abilities, so the body of Christ has many members with various gifts.

Numerous Scriptures speak of how Christ nurtures the church (Matt. 22:2; 25:1–13; John 10:1–16; 15:1–11; 1 Cor. 15:45; 2 Cor. 5:17; 11:2; Eph. 2:19–22; cf. 1 Cor. 3:11–15; 1 Peter 2:9; Rev. 1:6; cf. Heb. 8:1–6; Rev. 19:7–9) and speaks of the gifts which God gives the church (Rom. 12:6–8; 1 Cor. 12:4–31; Eph. 4:11–13). Some of these gifts were given only in the early church while others are still given today. The important central truth, however, is that every Christian is baptized by the Spirit and as such is a part of the body of Christ; and as a part of the body of Christ, he is given certain gifts that should be used in service for God.

The fact that Christians have been baptized into Christ and into His body means that they are identified with Him in that they have a new position in Christ. Because they are in Christ they receive the blessings that have been purchased for them by Christ's death on the cross. The new union described in the baptism of the Spirit unites them not only to Christ but to every other fellow believer and provides the important context of our relationship to other believers in this life as well as in the life to come. It is important to realize that all the tremendous work of the baptism of the Spirit occurs at the moment of saving faith and is never repeated subsequently in the Christian life.

The Indwelling of the Holy Spirit

Like the new birth and the baptism of the Spirit, the indwelling of the Holy Spirit comes to every Christian who is saved. Many Scriptures discuss the Spirit's indwelling (John 7:37–39; Acts 11:17; Rom. 5:5; 8:9, 11; 1 Cor. 2:12;

6:19–20; 12:13; 2 Cor. 5:5; Gal. 3:2; 4:6; 1 John 3:24; 4:13). The prominence of this doctrine in Scripture testifies to its importance in the life of a Christian, and the absence of the Holy Spirit is evidence that the person is not saved as stated in Romans 8:9: "You, however, are controlled not by the sinful nature but by the Spirit, if the Spirit of God lives in you. And if anyone does not have the Spirit of Christ, he does not belong to Christ."

Jesus described the Spirit of God as a gift from God in John 7:37–39: " 'If anyone is thirsty, let him come to me and drink. Whoever believes in me, as the Scripture has said, streams of living water will flow from within him.' By this he meant the Spirit, whom those who believe in him were later to receive. Up to that time the Spirit had not been given, since Jesus had not yet been glorified." In this prophecy Jesus anticipated the dramatic change that would occur on the day of Pentecost. While formerly the Holy Spirit did not indwell everybody who was born again, beginning at Pentecost everyone who was born again would have the Holy Spirit within him, who would constitute a source of the living water that Christ mentions. The contrast of the difference before and after Pentecost is stated by Christ in John 14:17: "But you know [the Spirit of Truth], for he lives with you [present] and will be in you [future]." Because a Christian under all the gracious provision of God is required to lead a holy life, the presence of the indwelling Holy Spirit will supply the supernatural enablement that will make this possible. It is important to note that even sinning Christians possess the indwelling Holy Spirit, and He does not leave a Christian once He is indwelling him. The challenge, however, is to let the Holy Spirit direct the life and fulfill the purpose of God in each individual.

Some passages have been misapplied, for instance, in the reference to the Spirit of God leaving Saul (1 Sam. 16:14). Prior to Pentecost not all believers were indwelt by the Spirit, and the Spirit of God could leave, as in the case of Saul, though this did not affect the issue of his new birth. Beginning at Pentecost, however, the Holy Spirit is the permanent possession of every believer. In a similar way, David's prayer in Psalm 51:11 requested God not to take the Spirit from him as He had from Saul. The departure of the Holy Spirit was a possibility in the Old Testament, though God did not take the Spirit from David. Likewise, in Luke 11:13 when the disciples asked for the Holy Spirit, it was still within the dispensation of the Old Testament in which the Holy Spirit was not given to all believers. The disciples, of course, would be indwelt by the Spirit on the day of Pentecost and, as a matter of fact, received the Spirit before Pentecost because Jesus breathed on them to give them divine enablement for their tasks (John 20:22).

Acts 5:32 states, "So is the Holy Spirit, whom God has given to those who obey him." Some have understood this to mean that perfect obedience is required for the indwelling. The obedience here, however, is not referring to moral commands but to the command to believe in Christ and be saved, which applied to every Christian. Once the command to believe has been obeyed, the Holy Spirit indwells that believer.

In Acts 8:14–20 a problem arose because some who were baptized by Philip had not received the Holy Spirit. In this case the indwelling of the Holy Spirit was delayed until Peter and John arrived and prayed for them that they would receive the Holy Spirit. The purpose of this was to identify the new Christians with the same Christians who received the Spirit on the day of Pentecost. The situation described here never occurred again.

One further reference is found in Acts 19:1–6 where followers of John the Baptist had not come in contact with the gospel about Jesus Christ. When the gospel was preached to them and they confessed their faith in Christ, they were immediately indwelt by the Spirit as manifested in this case by the speaking of tongues. Again, it was an experience that helped to connect early believers with the experience of the apostles on the day of Pentecost.

Some have had difficulty with the fact that the Holy Spirit is referred to as anointing believers. In the passages that occur in the New Testament, the anointing of the believers is synonymous with the indwelling of the Holy Spirit, and Christians are never exhorted to ask for anointing. Instead, because he is already indwelt and anointed, the Christian needs to be filled with the Spirit.

It is difficult to overestimate the importance of the indwelling of the Holy Spirit. To this can be added the evidence of John 14:23, which states that both the Father and the Son will also indwell the believer. In other words, all three Persons of the Trinity indwell every believer. Most of the ministry described in the New Testament, however, is on the part of the Holy Spirit as He enables a believer in Christ to lead a holy life and produce effective service.

The Holy Spirit as the Seal of God

Scripture refers to the fact that believers are sealed by the Holy Spirit. In 2 Corinthians 1:21–22 it is clear that the Holy Spirit's presence in the believer is God's seal: "Now it is God who makes both us and you stand firm in Christ. He anointed us, set his seal of ownership on us, and put his

Spirit in our hearts as a deposit, guaranteeing what is to come." A seal is the symbol of ownership. An important document received through the mail may be sealed to prevent tampering. The presence of the Holy Spirit indicates that we belong to God and have been set aside for safekeeping by God Himself until the day of redemption of our bodies, the day of resurrection. Like the indwelling of the Holy Spirit, the sealing of the Spirit made effective by His presence is universal among believers. According to Ephesians 4:30, Christians are "sealed for the day of redemption." This refers to the resurrection of the human body.

The fact that believers are sealed is another evidence that they are safe in the hands of God, and once they have received God's wonderful salvation, they can expect this to unfold in this life as well as in the life to come. As all the work of God in salvation is surveyed, it is clear that the moment a person is saved he is born again and receives new life in Christ, he is baptized into the body of Christ and into Christ, he is indwelt by the Holy Spirit as well as by God the Father and God the Son, and he is sealed by the presence of the Holy Spirit until the day of his resurrection.

Questions

1. What is meant by the "new birth"?
2. How did Jesus use the story of Moses and the pole with the bronze snake as an illustration of faith?
3. What other illustrations are used to describe the new birth?
4. Describe the new nature.
5. Does a believer still have his old nature after receiving the new nature?

6. When did spiritual baptism first take place?
7. What are the three major accomplishments for a believer when he is baptized by the Holy Spirit?
8. How would you contrast the baptism of the Spirit with the indwelling of the Spirit?
9. How would you contrast the baptism of the Spirit with the filling of the Spirit?
10. What is stated by the main text on the baptism of the Spirit?
11. Why is a Christian never urged to be baptized by the Spirit?
12. Describe how the body of Christ describes the church and the head of the body describes Christ.
13. Describe some ways in which Christ nurtures the church.
14. What gifts or special abilities are given to the church by the Holy Spirit?
15. How did Christ describe the gift of the Spirit in John 7:37–39? What are the prophesied results of the indwelling of the Holy Spirit?
16. Contrast the indwelling of the Holy Spirit after Pentecost to what was true before Pentecost as indicated by Christ in John 14:17.
17. How do you answer problems raised in certain passages such as 1 Samuel 16:14; Psalm 51:11; Luke 11:13; Acts 5:32; 8:14–20; and 19:1–6?
18. What evidence is there that all three Persons of the Trinity indwell the believer?
19. What is meant by the Holy Spirit as the seal of God?
20. How long will the seal of God keep us safe?

[9]

The Gifts of the Holy Spirit

The Permanent Gifts of the Spirit

IN THE NEW TESTAMENT God gave spiritual gifts, or the ability to perform spiritual tasks for the Lord. Some of these continue to exist today.

The Gift of Teaching. One of the important gifts is the gift of teaching (Rom. 12:7; 1 Cor. 12:28; Eph. 4:11). After individuals were saved and became part of the church, they needed to be taught; and some in the church were given special ability to teach spiritual truth. An effective teacher is one who is yielded to God, who is taught by the Holy Spirit, and who is able to interpret and apply the Word of God effectively. Today, teaching is limited to the teaching of the Old and New Testaments. An unsaved person may have a natural gift of teaching but would lack the ability to teach spiritual truth.

The Gift of Serving. Some Christians are also given the ability to serve, or help, in various ways (Rom. 12:7;

1 Cor. 12:28). Practically every Christian has the ability to help in some way, but all cannot be leaders. Accordingly, Romans 12:7 states, if a Christian's gift is serving, "Let him serve." Obviously, much of the Lord's work is manifest through helping or ministering.

The Gift of Administration. If one is given the gift of administration, or ruling (Rom. 12:8; 1 Cor. 12:28), he should "govern diligently." Not everybody can be a leader; not everybody has the gift of administration. Thus God gives some the ability to guide the church, and Christians who do not possess the gift of administration are exhorted to heed those who would administer the things of God and honor them by being obedient (Heb. 13:7).

The Gift of Evangelism. To the early church was given the gift of evangelism (Eph. 4:11), the ability to preach the gospel in such a way that souls are saved. All Christians, of course, are exhorted to spread the gospel. Timothy, who had the gift of a pastor, was exhorted to do the work of an evangelist even if his function was not exactly an exercise of that gift (2 Tim. 4:5).

The Gift of Pastor. One of the very important gifts in the early church was the gift of being a pastor (Eph. 4:11). The very word *pastor* refers to a shepherd who cares for his sheep. There is a similarity between what a shepherd does for his flock in caring for them, leading them, providing for them, and protecting them, and what a pastor does in relation to the church. It is of interest that in Ephesians 4:11 pastors are also linked to teachers, as if a good pastor is a teacher who feeds the flock through his teaching. By contrast, a teacher is not necessarily a pastor, but a pastor is always a teacher. Obviously, a shepherd who did not feed his flock would not be worthy of the name.

The Gift of Encouragement. The gift of encouragement (Rom. 12:8) has the thought of a special gift of admonishing and challenging people to do the work that God has given to them. It is, of course, directly related to the gift of getting people to do effective work for God.

The Gift of Giving. The gift of giving is a gift that every Christian should have to some extent. It is another gift of the Spirit (Rom. 12:8). Because a Christian is known by the way he handles his money in relationship to the Lord, every Christian should have a plan of stewardship that gives to the Lord proportionately as the Lord has blessed him. The gift of giving has in it the thought of being ready to give and being prompt in giving, and it is a work that is especially wrought in some Christians, though all Christians should exercise giving as a method of worship.

The Gift of Showing Mercy. Another gift is that of showing mercy (Rom. 12:8). This has in view mercy to the poor and needy and also to those in need of forgiveness.

The Gift of Faith. The gift of faith, as mentioned in 1 Corinthians 12:8–10, has the thought of a person who is implicit in his faith in the Word of God, who accepts the Bible for what it is—the very Word of God. While all Christians should have faith, some have a clearer and more effective faith than others, but it is a gift that should be desired.

Temporary Gifts of the Spirit

All of the gifts previously mentioned are gifts that exist today. There are some gifts, however, that many believe to be temporary, that is, they ceased after the apostolic age ended. In the lifetime of Christ and of the apostles, miracles occurred frequently that were designed to attest to the truthfulness of what they preached. The miracles of Christ testified to His deity; the miracles of the apostles testified to the truth of the gospel that they preached.

Though God can always perform miracles and does today, there was a decline in miracles as the church matured and the New Testament was written. The purpose of the miracles was to give credibility to the message that was given. Once the New Testament was completed, credibility was transferred to the Scripture itself, and the Scriptures are the authority by which one preaches the gospel today.

It is significant that in the Bible there were three notable periods of miracles, periods that began and ended. The first was the period of Moses and Joshua as the children of Israel were led from Egypt to the Promised Land. Daily they gathered the manna from heaven in the wilderness. They experienced water in the desert and God's protecting care over them in many ways. Once they were in the land, the manna ceased and the miracles that attended their journeys no longer existed. The miracles, however, gave credence to Moses and Joshua as God's appointed leaders and authenticated them in their roles as prophet and leader.

A second period of miracles is found in the time of Elijah and Elisha. This was in a period of Israel's apostasy, when the Word of God had been neglected. The miracles of Elijah and Elisha were to emphasize for the people of God that God did exist, that He was supernatural, that He was going to judge them, and that they should worship Him and obey Him. Once Elijah and Elisha passed from the scene, the special miracles that they performed ceased.

The third period of miracles in Scripture is that time in the New Testament during which Christ was on earth and the apostles lived and ministered. In this case, it was necessary for Christ to perform miracles as proof that He was indeed the Son of God in keeping with Old Testament predictions, and the apostles, likewise, performed miracles to demonstrate that they were operating in the power of God and that their message was from God. Once the New Testament was completed, however, this form of proof of credibility no longer was necessary as now the Bible itself could be quoted.

There is difference of opinion in the church today as to whether some of the gifts of the early church ceased or whether they continue. The true doctrine should be determined by the Bible itself rather than by human experience. It is obvious that the gifts of the early church are not being performed now in the same way they were.

The Gift of Apostleship. In the New Testament an apostle was one who was an official delegate, or one who operated under God's orders in being sent. The word *apostle* occurs about seventy-nine times in the New Testament and is found in numerous passages referring to the office of the twelve apostles (Matt. 10:2; Mark 3:14; 6:30; Luke 6:13). Certain individuals who were not of the Twelve were also called apostles as in the case of Paul (Rom. 1:1; 1 Cor. 1:1); Barnabas (Acts 14:14; cf. Gal. 2:9); Matthias (Acts 1:25–26); probably James (1 Cor. 15:7; Gal. 1:19); and Apollos (1 Cor. 4:6, 9). Several others are possibly classified as apostles: Silvanus and Timothy (1 Thess. 1:1; 2:6); Epaphroditus (Phil. 2:25, where he is called a "messenger" of Paul); some apostles who are not named (2 Cor. 8:23); and Andronicus and Junias (Rom. 16:7). Because the word "apostle" is used with various implications in these many references, those who were strictly apostles were those who had witnessed the Lord

Jesus Christ, which would include Paul, who had Christ revealed to him. Others, however, were sent and were God's official representatives even though they had not seen Christ visually.

Apostles were directly chosen by the Lord (Matt. 10:1–4; Mark 3:13–14; Luke 6:13; Acts 9:15–17; 13:2; 22:10, 14–15; Rom. 1:1). In addition to being chosen by God the apostles usually had miraculous powers or the ability to perform miracles (Matt. 10:1; Acts 5:15–16; 16:16–18; 28:8–9). The twelve apostles were given the special task of preaching the gospel and therefore had the keys of the kingdom, which is the gospel message (Matt. 10:7–8; 16:19). The twelve apostles were promised that in the future millennial kingdom they would judge the twelve tribes of Israel (Matt. 19:28). As the ministry of the church multiplied following Pentecost, apostles were commissioned especially to uncover the truth of the church then being revealed (Matt. 16:18; Eph. 3:1–12). Though the basic qualification was that they should be eyewitnesses of the Resurrection (Acts 1:22; 1 Cor. 9:1), it is obvious that some designated apostles were commissioned and given the gift without this experience.

It is important to note that apostleship is a gift of God, not something that is appointed by men (1 Cor. 12:28; Eph. 4:11). This is especially clear in 1 Corinthians 12:28, "And in the church God has appointed first of all apostles, second prophets, third teachers, then workers of miracles, also those having gifts of healing, those able to help others, those with gifts of administration, and those speaking in different kinds of tongues." There is no provision for the gift of apostleship to be continued, and no one has authority to bestow the office today.

The Gift of Prophecy. An important gift in the early

church was the gift of prophecy. This referred to people through whom God gave special divine revelation— sometimes about future events and sometimes about things that applied to the church currently. The gift of prophecy is mentioned in a number of passages (Rom. 12:6; 1 Cor. 12:10; 14:1–4). Some who are not designated as apostles were, nevertheless, prophets, such as Agabus (Acts 11:27–28). Also numbered among those who were prophets were Barnabas, Simeon, Lucius, Manaen, and Paul (Acts 13:1). Sometimes women had the gift of prophecy as indicated by the four daughters of Philip (Acts 21:9). And Paul had the gift of prophecy because his life manifested direct revelation from God (Acts 16:6–10; 18:9–11; 22:17–21; 27:23–24). Numbered among the prophets also were Judas and Silas (Acts 15:32). To exercise the prophetic office the prophet received a message from God and the ability to deliver that message clearly and accurately. The message as such had the authority of God.

Such direct revelation, however, was not necessary once the New Testament was written, but those in the apostolic church who did not have a New Testament needed guidance in doctrines that were very important to the church. Though the gift of teaching, or expounding the truth of the Word of God, is clearly given in the present age, today no one has received the gift of prophecy in the sense that he could add one word to the Scriptures or one truth that the Scripture does not contain. In Revelation 22:18–19 a solemn prohibition is leveled against any who would want to add to the Bible. God continues to give guidance to Christians seeking the will of God (Rom. 8:14), but such guidance is not a normative doctrine that could be added to God's Word.

The Gift of Miracles. God as God is able to perform

miracles in any age at any time suitable to His purpose. However, the gift of miracles mentioned in Scripture (1 Cor. 12:28) was a gift that was primarily used in the New Testament to authenticate the message that the apostles would preach. Though some believe that miracles are still valid, it is obvious that most of the work of God today is not accomplished on this basis but on the basis of the teaching and preaching of the written Word of God. While the gift of miracles may be considered as having ceased, God can continue to perform miracles in answer to prayer if He so chooses. But when a miracle is performed today, it is for a different purpose than that of authenticating the person who performs the miracle.

The Gift of Healing. In the New Testament numerous cases are displayed where people were healed, especially in the lifetime of Christ. In 1 Corinthians 12:9, 28, 30 healing is mentioned as a specific demonstration of the power of God. Such healing was beneficial to the human body and often corrected human ills that were unable to be cured by any other means.

God has not changed and miracles can be performed today, but it is questionable whether any individual has the gift of miracles, that is, the ability to heal all who come to him as was true in the case of Christ and of the apostles. Even in the book of Acts, however, healing was not as prominent a token of divine power as it was in the gospels.

The Gift of Tongues. In the church today there is a difference of opinion on whether or not tongues, as exercised in the early church, are given today as a spiritual gift.

The subject of tongues is not mentioned in the four gospels and only in Acts and 1 Corinthians in the rest of the New Testament. In the book of Acts speaking in tongues is mentioned three different times. The first time it is mentioned is on the day of Pentecost (Acts 2:1–13) when the eleven apostles and other believers present spoke in tongues that were not native to them. This event followed the advent of the Spirit of God, the indwelling of the church, and the filling of the Holy Spirit. The authentic character of this miracle was attested by the fact that people who were there from various countries found Christians speaking in languages that they knew but which were foreign to the persons speaking. Therefore, it made the impression that God was in it and testified to the truth of the gospel as it was being preached by Peter. It was also a partial fulfillment of Joel 2:29, where it was predicted that the Spirit would be poured forth, though it is not the complete fulfillment, which will yet await the period preceding the second coming of Christ.

In Acts 10:46 a second instance of speaking in tongues occurred in the case of Cornelius. Just as in Acts 2, where the demonstration of speaking in tongues was necessary to prove beyond doubt that the message was from God, so in Acts 10, when Peter preached the gospel to Gentiles, he was surprised that the Gentiles received the same gift as the apostles did on the day of Pentecost, and speaking in tongues was the evidence of it. It proved to Peter they were saved.

A third reference to speaking in tongues occurred in Acts 19:6, where some who had known only the baptism of John were introduced to the Christian faith and then spoke in tongues and prophesied.

Though speaking in tongues has been a controversial doctrine in the church today, it should be obvious in Scripture itself that tongues do not occupy a leading role in the early church's activities. Even though Paul claimed to have spoken in tongues, there is no instance where he used this as a method of preaching the gospel.

Whether or not one believes in tongues for today, the Scriptures are clear that there are certain regulations that govern the use of this gift. In 1 Corinthians 14 several principles are laid down: (1) Tongues were declared to be the least of the gifts and inferior to "strengthening, encouragement, and comfort" (1 Cor. 14:1–12). In this connection, Paul made the statement that five words of understanding were more important than ten thousand words in a tongue that is not understood (1 Cor. 14:19). (2) Tongues were to be used in the assembly only when the person speaking could interpret what he said (1 Cor. 14:13–20). (3) Tongues were intended to be a sign to unbelievers in fulfillment of prophecy (1 Cor. 14:22). Accordingly, it was not intended for the teaching of believers. (4) Speaking in tongues was to be regulated, and only two or three were permitted to speak in any one service, and then only if an interpreter was present (1 Cor. 14:26–38). It is probable that the gift of interpreting tongues also was a temporary gift; therefore, unless someone has this supernatural gift today, there should be no public speaking in tongues. (5) In a church assembly women were not to speak as a prophet or in tongues (1 Cor. 14:34–35). On the one hand, Paul recognized the validity of speaking in tongues in the apostolic period; on the other hand, other gifts were considered more important, those that minister directly to the edification of the church.

In summary, speaking in tongues is the least of the gifts; it is not a test of salvation today; it is not an indication of spirituality; and it is not inseparable from the baptism of the Spirit. These points are supported by the scriptural record concerning the use of tongues in the early church.

The Gift of Interpreting Tongues. The gift of interpreting tongues (1 Cor. 12:10; 14:26–28) was the ability to translate what others said in unknown tongues and give the meaning to the church. It is questionable whether anyone has the gift of interpretation today; and, if not, speaking in tongues would be limited to private exercise (1 Cor. 14:27).

The Gift of Discerning Spirits. In the early church it was quite necessary to distinguish between revelation from the Holy Spirit and deceitful revelation from Satan. Accordingly, some were given special gifts to discern truth from error (1 Cor. 12:10). There is a sense in which all Christians have some ability along this line as indicated in 1 John 2:27, "As for you, the anointing you received from him remains in you, and you do not need anyone to teach you. But as his anointing teaches you about all things and as that anointing is real, not counterfeit—just as it has taught you, remain in him." Inasmuch as every Christian is indwelt, or anointed, by the Spirit, to some extent he has the ability to distinguish truth from error. An important exercise of this is to test whether what others preach is the true gospel that Jesus Christ has come in the flesh (1 John 4:2) and attempt to determine whether the revelation comes from God (1 John 4:1).

The doctrine of the gifts of the Spirit is very important because it emphasizes how in the body of Christ different people have different gifts. No one has all the gifts, and all the gifts are not necessarily given to any particular person. The challenge is for each person who has spiritual gifts to exercise them in the power of the Holy Spirit and to use them for the purposes for which God has given them to him.

Questions

1. How would you define the gift of teaching?
2. How would you contrast the natural gift of teaching and the spiritual gift of teaching?

3. How would you define the gift of serving?

4. What is the gift of administration?

5. What is the significance of the fact that not every Christian has the gift of administration?

6. What is the gift of evangelism?

7. Is it possible for one who does not have the gift of evangelism to preach the gospel of salvation?

8. What is the gift of pastor? How does it relate to the shepherd's caring for his sheep?

9. What is the significance of linking pastors and teachers in Ephesians 4:11?

10. How would you define the gift of encouragement?

11. What is the gift of giving?

12. What is the gift of showing mercy?

13. What is the gift of faith?

14. What is the distinction between permanent spiritual gifts and temporary spiritual gifts?

15. Why were miracles necessary in the lifetime of Christ?

16. Can God always perform miracles? Does He do it today?

17. What was the purpose of the miracles in the New Testament?

18. Name the three notable periods of miracles, when they started, and when they stopped.

19. From the fact that previous periods of miracles stopped, can we draw a lesson concerning the ending of the third period of miracles?

20. What is the gift of apostleship? Is it given today?

21. Who gives the gift of apostleship?

22. How is the gift of prophecy to be defined?

23. Were all Christians prophets?

24. What is the gift of miracles?

25. How is the gift of miracles contrasted with the capacity of God to still perform miracles today?

26. What is the gift of healing?
27. Does anyone have the gift of healing today?
28. How is the gift of tongues defined?
29. Name three incidents in the book of Acts where tongues are mentioned.
30. Are tongues ever mentioned in the four gospels or in the epistles of Paul, except in 1 Corinthians?
31. If tongues are used today, what are some of the principles concerning its limitations?
32. What is the evidence that speaking in tongues was genuine in Acts 2?
33. Why was the gift of tongues exercised in Acts 10?
34. Why was the gift of tongues exercised in Acts 19:6?
35. How prominent was the speaking in tongues in the preaching of the gospel, such as Paul's preaching?
36. What can we conclude by the statement that tongues are the least of the gifts?
37. What is the implication that tongues should be used only when an interpreter is present?
38. What was the purpose of the gift of tongues?
39. How often should people be allowed to speak in tongues in a given church service?
40. Were women allowed to speak in tongues in the church services?
41. How would you summarize the biblical teaching on the gift of tongues?
42. What is the gift of interpreting tongues?
43. What is the gift of discerning spirits?
44. Are all the gifts necessarily given to any one particular person?
45. What is the challenge to each person who has spiritual gifts?

[10]

The Filling of the Holy Spirit

Definition of the Filling of the Spirit

CHRISTIANS ARE DISTINGUISHED from non-Christians as those who have been born again, who have received eternal life, who are baptized into the body of Christ, who are indwelt by the Holy Spirit, and who are sealed by the Holy Spirit. These works of the Spirit are evident in any true Christian.

It is obvious, however, that all Christians do not have the same degree of spirituality, or wisdom, or yieldedness to the Lord. Accordingly, the Scriptures speak of those who are spiritual and those who are fleshly, living in the power and direction of the sin nature. The Corinthians who were addressed in 1 Corinthians 1:2 as "those sanctified in Christ Jesus and called to be holy, together with all those everywhere who call on the name of our Lord Jesus Christ—their Lord and ours" are nevertheless classified as either spiritual or worldly. First Corinthians 3:1 states,

"Brothers, I could not address you as spiritual but as worldly—mere infants in Christ." How can one define the difference between a Christian who is spiritual and one who is not?

The difference is related to the work of the Holy Spirit in a person's heart. Every Christian is indwelt by the Spirit, but every Christian does not heed the direction and instruction of the Holy Spirit. Accordingly, those who listen to the world rather than to the Holy Spirit are worldly, or fleshly, and those who are guided by the Holy Spirit can be spiritually minded and enjoy the things of God. Those who are spiritual "live by the Spirit" (Gal. 5:16), that is, they walk, or live their life, in the power of the Holy Spirit.

Christians who have been saved for a long period of time often achieve spiritual maturity when they have grown in grace and in the knowledge of the Lord (2 Peter 3:18). Spiritual growth toward maturity is revealed in Ephesians 4:11–16:

It was he who gave some to be apostles, some to be prophets, some to be evangelists, and some to be pastors and teachers, to prepare God's people for works of service, so that the body of Christ may be built up until we all reach unity in the faith and in the knowledge of the Son of God and become mature, attaining to the whole measure of the fullness of Christ. Then we will no longer be infants, tossed back and forth by the waves, and blown here and there by every wind of teaching and by the cunning and craftiness of men in their deceitful scheming. Instead, speaking the truth in love, we will in all things grow up into him who is the Head, that is, Christ. From him the whole body, joined and held together by every supporting ligament, grows and builds itself up in love, as each part does its work.

Spiritual maturity, however, is not measured by the length of time that one is a Christian, but rather by the extent a Christian grows in the knowledge and fellowship of the Lord. It is possible even for a new Christian to be filled with the Spirit, as illustrated a number of times in Scripture.

In the Old Testament the filling of the Spirit was rare and was usually related to the ability to serve in some particular area. Sinning against God was defined in the Old Testament as grieving the Spirit (Isa. 63:10–11; cf. Eph. 4:30). Undoubtedly, the Spirit of God was behind the work of the inspiration of the Old Testament, and those who wrote Scripture were guided infallibly in what they wrote. The Spirit of God in the Old Testament gave men wisdom (Gen. 41:38–40; Num. 27:18; Judg. 3:10; 6:34; 11:29; 1 Sam. 10:10; 16:13). The Holy Spirit also gave men special skills in the Old Testament, such as the tailors for the priestly garments (Ex. 28:3) and the workmen who built the tabernacle (Ex. 31:3; cf. 35:30–35). In the case of Samson, the Holy Spirit's filling gave him superhuman strength (Judg. 13:25; 14:6, 19; 15:14). It is probable that the Holy Spirit was involved in the miracles of the Old Testament, though they are not attributed to the Holy Spirit specifically.

In the New Testament the filling of the Spirit takes on more of a work of God on behalf of the spirituality of the individual Christian. In the Old Testament the filling of the Spirit seems to be sovereignly given, while in the New Testament the Holy Spirit was given to those who were spiritually yielded to God. The filling of the Holy Spirit is frequently attached to some utterance in which the Spirit of God used individuals to express the truth of God. Elizabeth, the mother of John the Baptist, was said to have been filled with the Holy Spirit (Luke 1:41). Zechariah also was filled with the Spirit at the time of John's birth (Luke 1:67).

Most of the references concerning the filling of the Spirit occur in the New Testament. In Acts 2:2–4 those assembled were filled with the Spirit. When Peter was called before the Sanhedrin concerning his testimony for Christ, Scripture states that he was filled with the Holy Spirit (Acts 4:8). The group of Christians who met together for prayer following this incident were filled with the Spirit (Acts 4:31). In Acts 9:17 shortly after his conversion, Paul was said to be filled with the Spirit. Paul again was filled with the Spirit according to Acts 13:9. From these many instances it is obvious that a person is filled with the Spirit when he is under the control and is empowered by the Holy Spirit. In the Old Testament this was sovereignly given and was not available for everyone.

In the New Testament Christians are challenged and commanded to be filled with the Spirit, as it states in Ephesians 5:18, "Do not get drunk on wine, which leads to debauchery. Instead, be filled with the Spirit." The illustration of a person whose whole body has been affected by wine is used to describe how the Spirit of God, who indwells every believer, can extend His ministry and His power to all aspects of an individual Christian's life. The filling of the Spirit is not getting more of the Spirit, but it is a question of the Holy Spirit empowering and getting control. In contrast to the permanence of the new birth and the indwelling Holy Spirit, the filling of the Spirit is a repeated experience. That is why Ephesians 5:18 translated literally is "keep being filled." Peter, who was filled on the day of Pentecost, was said to be filled again in Acts 4:8. The martyr Stephen was filled with the Spirit before he was

killed (Acts 7:55). Paul and Barnabas were filled with the
Spirit a number of times (Acts 9:17; 11:24; 13:8–52).

Conditions for Being Filled with the Spirit

Though all Christians are equally saved, not all
Christians are equally filled with the Spirit. The epistles of
Paul contain exhortations to us to meet the conditions of
the filling of the Holy Spirit. In 1 Thessalonians 5:19 the
command is given, "Do not put out the Spirit's fire."
Speaking of the Holy Spirit as a fire within us, Christians
are exhorted not to quench Him or suffocate Him. In the
King James Version it is translated "quench not the Spirit."

When we are saved we recognize that Jesus Christ is
the Son of God and that God is saving us. However, the
full implications of putting our faith in God usually come
later when we face the issue of whether Christ is really the
Lord of our life. As Christ expressed it in the Sermon on
the Mount, "No one can serve two masters. Either he will
hate the one and love the other, or he will be devoted to the
one and despise the other" (Matt. 6:24). This is true as
Christ stated, "You cannot serve both God and Money"
(Matt. 6:24). Accordingly, a number of times Christians are
exhorted in the Scriptures to yield themselves wholly to
God. In Romans 6:13 the exhortation is given, "Do not
offer the parts of your body to sin, as instruments of
wickedness, but rather offer yourselves to God, as those
who have been brought from death to life; and offer the
parts of your body to him as instruments of righteousness."
The concept is that of offering our bodies as a living
sacrifice in contrast to offering a sacrifice of something
dead. The two options before Christians are whether we
should serve God or whether we should serve wickedness.
The verb translated "Do not offer the parts of your body to

sin" (Rom. 6:13) is in the present tense. In other words, we should not keep on doing this as Christians, but, as he states, "rather offer yourselves to God." Here the verb is in the aorist tense, which has the thought of doing it once and for all. Accordingly, the exhortation is to stop doing what we are doing wrong and to take a decisive step in allowing our members to be used for righteousness.

A similar truth is stated in Romans 12:1–2. There Paul writes, "I urge you, brothers, in view of God's mercy, to offer your bodies as living sacrifices, holy and pleasing to God—this is your spiritual act of worship. Do not conform any longer to the pattern of this world, but be transformed by the renewing of your mind. Then you will be able to test and approve what God's will is—his good, pleasing and perfect will." In this passage, as in Romans 6:13, the thought is to present ourselves to God once and for all as a specific act. Presenting or offering ourselves to God takes the form of a living sacrifice. Because we are saved, we have been prepared to do this because God has declared that such a sacrifice is "holy and pleasing to God."

Having taken this step, Christians are to continue in their spiritual lives by being transformed in their minds, enabling them to detect what God's will is for their lives. The secret of determining God's will for our lives is to yield to God wholly first, and then God is free to reveal what He wants us to do.

Therefore, we should not put out the Spirit's fire or quench the Spirit, but we must present our bodies as a living sacrifice to the Lord. This is viewed as a once-for-all act of committing one's self to the Lord.

A second command, however, is given in Ephesians 4:30. There Christians are commanded, "Do not grieve the

Holy Spirit of God, with whom you were sealed for the day of redemption."

Unfortunately, in human experience it is difficult to be holy and to continue at all times in situations entirely surrendered to the Lord. When sin enters the life of a Christian, the Holy Spirit is hindered in His ministry and He is "grieved."

The remedy for this situation is confession as stated in 1 John 1:9, "If we confess our sins, he is faithful and just and will forgive us our sins and purify us from all unrighteousness." Because a Christian has already been saved, justified, and promised fellowship with Christ in eternity, when sin enters his experience, confession is the secret of cleansing from this sin. Unfortunately, few Christians have faced these important doctrinal distinctives; they have not fully yielded themselves to God and have not fully confessed their sins to the Lord. In forgiving a Christian, God is not simply acting mercifully, He is acting justly because Christ has paid the price for our sins and has made it possible for God to restore those to fellowship who have fallen short.

Scriptures warn, however, that if a Christian continues in sin and continues to grieve the Holy Spirit he can experience God's chastening judgment. This is introduced in connection with the Lord's Supper in 1 Corinthians 11:31–32: "If we judged ourselves, we would not come under judgment. When we are judged by the Lord, we are being disciplined so that we will not be condemned with the world." In the previous context (1 Cor. 11:27–30), Paul reveals that if one continues to sin against God, it can result in physical illness or even death. It is, therefore, a dangerous thing for a Christian to live outside the will of God. God is gracious, however, and in many cases does not immediately deal with the matter. But eventually the Christian has to face his departure from God and adjust his relationship to the Lord.

Another passage dealing with this is Hebrews 12:5–6, "You have forgotten that word of encouragement that addresses you as sons: 'My son, do not make light of the Lord's discipline, and do not lose heart when he rebukes you, because the Lord disciplines those he loves, and he punishes everyone he accepts as a son.' " As Hebrews makes clear, God may discipline a Christian who has wandered from the path of righteousness. Christians are assured that if they do not confess their sin, God will move in and discipline them for their shortcomings. Through this entire process, however, it is clear that the Christian remains saved because he is saved by grace and not by works; but he will not enjoy his salvation to the full if he is not yielded to God's Spirit, and he will lose fruit in eternity.

Living by the Spirit

In contrasting a life with God in the power of the Spirit to a life of sin, the apostle Paul establishes a simple principle when he says, "Live by the Spirit, and you will not gratify the desires of the sinful nature" (Gal. 5:16). Literally translated, he says "walk by the Spirit." The Christian's life is like a walk where each step is a step of faith and each step that is taken needs to be sustained by strong limbs. Likewise, a Christian who is living by faith is walking a step at a time. In his own strength a believer cannot lead a Christian life; he needs the sustaining power of the Holy Spirit each step he takes. A Christian is warned against fulfilling the desires of the sinful nature, and the acts of the sinful nature are itemized in Galatians 5:19–21.

Accordingly, the spiritual life and the life of being filled with the Spirit involve not resisting or quenching the Holy Spirit, not grieving the Holy Spirit by unconfessed sin, but walking by faith in the Holy Spirit. Because of the high standard of a Christian's spiritual life as revealed in the New Testament, walking by the Spirit is the secret of a spiritual life that bears testimony to the reality and power of God and is effective for Him.

A Christian has to face evil on various fronts. The world and the world system constantly are attempting to choke the Christian and to divert him to things that have no eternal value. Worldliness will choke the Word and make it unfruitful (Matt. 13:22). Instead, the Christian should view sin through the cross of Christ, as Paul did, which kept him from temptations of the world (Gal. 6:14). A Christian also faces the power of Satan, and many times in the New Testament the truth of Satan's antagonism and temptations are mentioned. As Paul states in Ephesians 6:12, "Our struggle is not against flesh and blood, but against the rulers, against the authorities, against the powers of this dark world and against the spiritual forces of evil in the heavenly realms."

Behind the scene and not seen by the natural eye is the continued work of Satan seeking to destroy the Christian. In 1 Peter 5:8–9 Christians are exhorted, "Be self-controlled and alert. Your enemy the devil prowls around like a roaring lion looking for someone to devour. Resist him, standing firm in the faith, because you know that your brothers throughout the world are undergoing the same kind of sufferings." In the spiritual struggle, all Christians face a world system that is contrary to the things of God, the power of Satan to tempt us to sin, and a sin nature that wants to lead us back to the old life. The Holy Spirit and

His power is the secret of victory as the Christian yields to Him and allows the Holy Spirit to lead and direct.

The Effect of Being Filled with the Holy Spirit

In the New Testament it is clear that the entire work of God on behalf of the believer is related to the question of whether he is filled with the Spirit. A number of important results come when a person is filled with the Spirit.

Progressive Sanctification. When a person is saved, he is set apart as holy to God, and this justifies the use of the word "saint" which means "set apart for holy use." Even in the case of sinning Christians, they are regarded as saints in Scripture. It is God's purpose, however, that what is true of every Christian in regard to his *position* as a saint be made effective in his spiritual *state* so that progressively he is sanctified and becomes more and more like God. The night before His crucifixion Jesus prayed, "Sanctify them by the truth; your word is truth" (John 17:17). The important experience of becoming a Spirit-filled Christian results in the progressive sanctification of a believer in Christ. The result will be that he will manifest the fruit of the Spirit as stated in Galatians 5:22–23, "But the fruit of the Spirit is love, joy, peace, patience, kindness, goodness, faithfulness, gentleness and self-control. Against such things there is no law." The filling of the Spirit produces this character-transforming fruit which should be true of every Christian. This fruit is made possible by the filling of the Spirit and the believer's living union with Christ (cf. John 15:5; 1 Cor. 12:12–13).

Empowering Spiritual Gifts. The effect of being filled with the Spirit not only transforms a Christian's character but also empowers his spiritual gifts. One of these is the gift of teaching. Christ predicted that His disciples would teach the truth (John 16:12–15), using the Word of God as inspired by the Holy Spirit. As the Spirit of God serves as a teacher to the one who wants to teach, He will guide him into all truth. This is made clear in John 16:12–13, "I have much more to say to you, more than you can now bear. But when he, the Spirit of truth, comes, he will guide you into all truth. He will not speak on his own; he will speak only what he hears, and he will tell you what is yet to come."

Guidance of the Spirit. Another important result of being filled with the Spirit is that the Christian can experience the guidance of God. The matter of guidance comes in where the Word of God is not specific. Christians need guidance in specific decisions that relate to their life and service. As mentioned earlier in Romans 12:1–2, once one is a living sacrifice, he then can be guided into what is God's perfect will. An illustration of this is the servant of Abraham seeking a wife for Isaac in Genesis 24:27, which states, "Praise be to the LORD, the God of my master Abraham, who has not abandoned his kindness and faithfulness to my master. As for me, the LORD has led me on the journey to the house of my master's relatives." This illustration indicates that the servant did what he could with information that was in his possession, namely, he went to the family where Rebekah lived, but he needed specific guidance concerning the selection of Isaac's future wife. Christians who are walking with the Lord experience guidance in their decisions, and this is one of the evidences that their relationship to God is real. Romans 8:14 states, "Those who are led by the Spirit of God are sons of God."

Assurance of Salvation. Another important aspect in Christian experience is the doctrine of assurance, that is, the Spirit of God's working in the life of a yielded

Christian can bear witness to the fact that he is actually a child of God. Romans 8:16 says, "The Spirit himself testifies with our spirit that we are God's children." It is God's intent to assure those who have put their trust in Christ that they are saved and that they can expect God's salvation to carry them through into eternity. The truth of assurance of salvation is also mentioned in Galatians 4:6, 1 John 3:24, and in 1 John 4:13.

Worship. The act of worship is also a work of the Spirit in the life of a yielded believer. Following the command to be filled with the Spirit, Paul mentions that the Spirit-filled believer should exercise worship of God, "Speak to one another with psalms, hymns and spiritual songs. Sing and make music in your heart to the Lord, always giving thanks to God the Father for everything, in the name of our Lord Jesus Christ" (Eph. 5:19–20).

Intercession of the Holy Spirit. Christians also need help in their prayer lives because often we do not know what we should pray for. In this respect, the Holy Spirit intercedes for us: "In the same way, the Spirit helps us in our weakness. We do not know what we ought to pray for, but the Spirit himself intercedes for us with groans that words cannot express" (Rom. 8:26). A major area of ministry of the Holy Spirit is to enable a Christian to serve the Lord. Though believers may have some natural gifts, to be used of God in spiritual service it is necessary for His servants to be guided and empowered by the Holy Spirit. Christ anticipated this when He predicted that "streams of living water will flow from within [the Spirit-filled believer]" (John 7:38). It is not too much to say that the Holy Spirit of God is the key to effective Christian life and service, and apart from His ministry to us, the Christian life is fruitless and empty.

Questions

1. How are Christians distinguished from non-Christians?
2. How are Christians classified according to their spiritual life?
3. How is the spiritual life related to the indwelling Holy Spirit?
4. How do you contrast spiritual maturity and spiritual life?
5. What was the nature of the filling of the Spirit in the Old Testament?
6. How does the Old Testament distinguish those who were sinning against God and those who were yielded to God?
7. How is the Holy Spirit related to the inspiration of the Scripture?
8. How is the Holy Spirit related to having wisdom?
9. How is the Spirit of God related to special skills?
10. How does the New Testament differ from the Old on the subject of the filling of the Spirit?
11. What are some instances of the filling of the Spirit in the Gospels?
12. What was the first time that an assembly was filled with the Spirit?
13. What were some of the instances of the filling of the Spirit in the book of Acts?
14. How does drinking wine serve as an illustration of the filling of the Spirit?
15. Does a person who is filled with the Spirit get more of the Spirit?
16. Can the Spirit of God fill a person more than once?
17. What does the exhortation of 1 Thessalonians 5:19 mean in relation to being filled with the Spirit?

18. Explain the option that is before Christians indicated in Matthew 6:24 and Romans 6:13.

19. How does Romans 12:1–2 fit into the picture of the spiritual life?

20. What are the conditions for discovering the will of God?

21. What is meant by "grieving the Spirit of God"?

22. What is the remedy for grieving the Spirit of God?

23. How is spiritual life related to the Lord's Supper?

24. What should a Christian's attitude be when the Lord disciplines him?

25. What does it mean to live by the Spirit?

26. How is living by the Spirit illustrated by walking?

27. In view of the high standards of the Christian life, what is God's provision for the spiritual life?

28. How does worldliness choke the Spirit of God?

29. How does Satan deal with a Christian?

30. How should we deal with Satan's temptations?

31. How does the spiritual life relate to progressive sanctification?

32. How is the fruit of the Spirit achieved?

33. What is the relation of the filling of the Spirit to spiritual gifts?

34. What is the relation of the filling of the Spirit to guidance?

35. What is the relation of the filling of the Spirit to assurance of salvation?

36. What is the relation of the filling of the Spirit to worship?

37. What is the intercession of the Holy Spirit? Why is it necessary?

38. How would you summarize the importance of the indwelling Holy Spirit in relation to the Christian's life and service?

[11]

Spiritual Power

Man's Inadequacy

THOSE WHO BECOME CHRISTIANS by faith in Christ soon discover that being born again does not automatically solve all their spiritual problems. Satan, who has done everything he can to keep a person from becoming a Christian, now changes his tactics to keeping a Christian from achieving a real testimony for Christ.

1. The Christian is faced with a world system that is contrary to serving the Lord. The world's standards, its values, its immorality, and its materialism constitute a formidable opposition to a Christian who wants to serve the Lord effectively.

2. Satan also will do all he can to keep a Christian from fulfilling God's plan for his life. Christians, accordingly, are exhorted to "be self-controlled and alert. Your enemy the devil prowls around like a roaring lion looking for someone to devour. Resist him, standing firm in the faith, because you know that your brothers

throughout the world are undergoing the same kind of sufferings" (1 Peter 5:8–9).

3. In addition to satanic opposition, which can be very real in a Christian's life, we still have a sin nature. Even though we are born again and have a new nature in Christ, the sin nature resists the desires and goals of the new nature. What we were before we were saved tends to draw us back into the old life, which does not honor Christ. This is not a peculiar problem for some Christians; it is a problem for all Christians. The apostle Paul speaks of this when he states, "I know that nothing good lives in me, that is, in my sinful nature. For I have the desire to do what is good, but I cannot carry it out. For what I do is not the good I want to do; no, the evil I do not want to do—this I keep on doing. Now if I do what I do not want to do, it is no longer I who do it, but it is sin living in me that does it" (Rom. 7:18–20). After further discussion of this problem, Paul concludes "What a wretched man I am! Who will rescue me from this body of death? Thanks be to God—through Jesus Christ our Lord!" (Rom. 7:24–25).

The answer to this inadequacy of human beings to solve their own problems, even after they are saved, is found in God's provision for power over sin and the power to have victory in Christ. To accomplish the purpose of a Christian leading a holy life, God has made rich provision.

The Power of the Holy Spirit

The Holy Spirit indwells every Christian, and because He is God and has all the power of God, He is able to help a Christian to overcome his inadequacy and to have a life and testimony that is honoring to God. The secret of drawing on His power is one of faith so that we live by the Spirit. Paul wrote to the believers in Galatia saying, "Live by the Spirit, and you will not gratify the desires of the sinful nature. For the sinful nature desires what is contrary to the Spirit, and the Spirit what is contrary to the sinful nature. They are in conflict with each other, so that you do not do what you want. But if you are led by the Spirit, you are not under the law" (Gal. 5:16–18).

Living by the Spirit is depending moment by moment on the power of the Spirit to overcome our own inadequacy. Christians need to realize that within them is the omnipotence of God and that there is no problem that God cannot solve. Accordingly, the life of victory is a life of faith as we live day by day, relying on the Holy Spirit to give us power to serve the Lord effectively.

Today airplanes provide rapid transportation from one place to another. It is possible to get on a plane and travel thousands of miles in just a few hours. The secret, however, is trusting the plane enough to get on board and let the plane carry you. Likewise, a Christian faces the impossible task of honoring God on his own, but as he rests in the power of the Holy Spirit, the Spirit of God can support him and carry him moment by moment in his service and testimony for the Lord. It is impossible for a believer to achieve what he should by way of obedience and commitment to God without relying upon the power of the Holy Spirit.

The Power of the Word of God

In addition to what God provides by the indwelling presence of the Holy Spirit, the Bible with its infinite revelation of God is available to Christians. One of the ministries of the Holy Spirit is to teach us the Word of God and to acquaint us with the facts of God's provisions for our needs as well as God's standards and values.

In the epistle to the Hebrews, the power of the Word of God is described, "For the word of God is living and active. Sharper than any doubled-edged sword, it penetrates even to dividing soul and spirit, joints and marrow; it judges the thoughts and attitudes of the heart" (Heb. 4:12). The Bible provides a most essential avenue of communication of God to us. In it He declares infinite truths that acquaint us with God and His purposes in the world. The Word of God, because it is such an accurate presentation of the truth of God, serves to purify and to guide.

The psalmist asked the question, "How can a young man keep his way pure?" (Ps. 119:9). The same verse gives us the answer, "By living according to your word." Knowledge of the Word of God and the availability of divine power does much for a Christian and enables him to lead the kind of a Christian life that will be an honor to God. The psalmist states, "Your word is a lamp to my feet and a light for my path" (Ps. 119:105). In the darkness of the night a lamp will show enough of the path ahead to guide us in the next step. The Word of God is like that. It may not give us guidance regarding ten years from now, but it does give us guidance concerning what we should do day by day. In addition to the Word of God itself, the Holy Spirit interprets the Word and applies it to our particular need and gives us even more direct instruction.

Scriptures are a work of the Holy Spirit. As stated in 2 Timothy 3:16–17, "All Scripture is God-breathed and is useful for teaching, rebuking, correcting and training in righteousness, so that the man of God may be thoroughly equipped for every good work." As this passage states, the Holy Spirit teaches us the truth we need. It rebukes us if we have transgressed the Law of God. It provides a way of correction and shows how we should be living, and then it gives us training in how to live a righteous life before God. The result would be that if the Word of God has its full effect upon us, the individual Christian is equipped for the work that God has called him to do.

The blessed man described in Psalm 1:2–3 is the one who meditates upon the Word of God, "But his delight is in the law of the LORD, and on his law he meditates day and night. He is like a tree planted by streams of water, which yields its fruit in season and whose leaf does not wither. Whatever he does prospers." Just as a tree planted near water can draw water and prosper even when the rest of the area is dry, so a Christian living in a world that does not support his spiritual life can draw upon the deep springs of the Word of God and in that truth be able to live above the standards of the world. Christians soon discover the necessity of reading the Bible every day. It is important to have a daily appointment with God to read the Bible and to pray and, if possible, to make it a family practice.

In Scripture there is a revelation of who God is, His holiness and righteousness, His infinity, His omniscience, His omnipresence, His love and grace. The Bible also reveals who man is—that he was created in the likeness of God but fell through willful sin. Man is capable, however, of receiving the transforming grace of God, and those who put their trust in Christ begin the process of sanctification that ultimately will present them perfect in the presence of God. The Bible outlines God's philosophy of history, including His program for the Gentile nations as illustrated in the book of Daniel, His program for Israel in the past, present, and future, His program for the church, and His warning of the future of the unsaved. The Bible is the timeless book that meets our current needs and helps us to achieve the utmost in a godly life and useful service for God.

The Power of the Blood of Christ

The Bible also speaks of the power of the blood of Christ that was shed upon the cross. The fact that the blood of Christ was shed assures us of the power of God to forgive sin. This is stated in Hebrews 9:22, "The law requires that nearly everything be cleansed with blood, and without the shedding of blood there is no forgiveness." It is through the blood of Christ that we have redemption (Eph. 1:7; Rev. 5:9). Through the shed blood of Christ we receive propitiation, or satisfaction before God, so that our sins may be forgiven (Rom. 3:25). The blood of Christ has the power to cleanse us from sin.

This is the argument of Hebrews 9:13–14, "The blood of goats and bulls and the ashes of a heifer sprinkled on those who are ceremonially unclean sanctify them so that they are outwardly clean. How much more, then, will the blood of Christ, who through the eternal Spirit offered himself unblemished to God, cleanse our consciences from acts that lead to death, so that we may serve the living God!"

Our cleansing is not through a redemption purchased with silver and gold but with the precious blood of Christ as stated in 1 Peter 1:18–19, "You know that it was not with perishable things such as silver or gold that you were redeemed from the empty way of life handed down to you from your forefathers, but with the precious blood of Christ, a lamb without blemish or defect." The power of the death of Christ, as stated in these many passages that refer to the blood of Christ shed for us, is one of the important aspects of God's process of sanctification of a believer. As we contemplate the death of Christ and all He did for us, it serves to remind us of God's holy purpose and His desire that we might be examples of His righteousness even in our daily lives.

The Power of Prayer

One of the great privileges given to a Christian as a child of God is his access to the throne of God in heaven. Again and again in Scripture the Christian is reminded that he can come to God with his petitions and expect God to hear and answer. Christ reminded His disciples frequently of this. On the night before His crucifixion He told them, "If you remain in me and my words remain in you, ask whatever you wish, and it will be given you" (John 15:7). Later the same evening Christ said, "I tell you the truth, my Father will give you whatever you ask in my name" (John 16:23).

In offering prayer to God, it is important to ask in the name of Christ. As Jesus told His own disciples, "I will do whatever you ask in my name, so that the Son may bring glory to the Father. You may ask me for anything in my name, and I will do it" (John 14:13–14). Jesus also said, "In that day you will no longer ask me anything. I tell you the truth, my Father will give you whatever you ask in my name" (John 16:23).

Asking in the name of Christ implies that it is God's will. This is stated more clearly in 1 John 5:14–15, "This is the confidence we have in approaching God: that if we ask anything according to his will, he hears us. And if we know that he hears us—whatever we ask—we know that we have what we asked of him."

Prayer is not a means by which a believer receives something contrary to the will of God. It is rather the means by which God miraculously brings into a believer's life that which he requested in prayer according to His will.

Some companies that write checks today require two signatures, and the check is only good when both signatures are affixed. Likewise, in our prayer life we send our petitions to God and sign the check. We then send it to Jesus Christ. If He signs it, it does not make any difference how great or impossible it is—that prayer will be answered in keeping with what has been asked.

It is a fact of human experience that sometimes God does not seem to answer prayer, and this may indicate that our prayer has not been according to the will of God. It is also true that sometimes God will answer our prayer, but not immediately. For this reason we need to keep on praying. God in His own time and in His own way will fulfill our request even as He honors and glorifies Himself in our prayer life. This, of course, is all that an intelligent, God-fearing Christian would desire. Once we have presented our petitions to God, we can rest in God's answer even if no apparent answer is received. Now that our request has been made, the problem remaining is in the will of God, at least for the present.

The Power of Christ's Intercession

An important aspect of the prayer of believers is the fact that Christ is in heaven interceding for us. According to Hebrews 7:25 Christ "is able to save completely those who come to God through him, because he always lives to intercede for them." Because God is infinite, He is able to give His full attention to one believer without detracting from His attention to another. It is a marvelous truth of Scripture that God continuously gives His attention to us, and Christ is interceding on our behalf. When believers pray to God, they are joining a prayer meeting already in session, and the object of their prayers is to fulfill and coincide with what God desires for them.

Scriptures also make clear that sometimes believers do not receive answers to prayer because they do not ask or they ask from the wrong motives. As James expresses it, "When you ask, you do not receive, because you ask with wrong motives, that you may spend what you get on your pleasures" (James 4:3). James also expresses the problem of failing to pray, "You do not have, because you do not ask God" (James 4:2). The challenge in the prayer life, accordingly, is to ask and present our needs to God, but to ask with the right motives and with the right goals. If we ask according to the will of God in the name of Christ, our prayers will be answered. In addition to moment-by-moment fellowship with God, we need stated times for daily prayer.

Appropriating the spiritual power that God has provided is an important factor in a believer's life and service. In view of his own inadequacy, he needs the power of the Holy Spirit, the power of the Word of God, the power of the blood of Christ, the power of prayer, and the power of Christ's intercession. God has richly provided, and Christians should avail themselves by faith of what God has provided in His grace for a Christian's life.

Questions

1. Is it normal for Christians to realize that they are inadequate in themselves to solve their spiritual problems?
2. What is the effect of the world's system upon a Christian?

3. What is Satan's desire in regard to a Christian?

4. Define the problem of the sin nature, explaining how it relates to the new nature received in the new birth.

5. What is the secret of gaining victory over the sin nature?

6. How does the Holy Spirit relate to a believer's inadequacy?

7. How can the Christian draw on the power of the Holy Spirit?

8. How does flying in an airplane illustrate the Christian life?

9. Explain why it is impossible for a Christian in his own power to lead a Christian life.

10. How is the Word of God described in its relationship to a believer in Hebrews 4:12?

11. How does the Word of God affect a person's purity? And how does it serve as a guide for a Christian's life? How does a lamp illustrate this?

12. According to 2 Timothy 3:16–17, what can we expect that the Scriptures will accomplish in our lives?

13. How is the blessed man of Psalm 1 an illustration of how a Christian can draw from the unseen power of God?

14. To what extent does the Bible provide God's philosophy of history?

15. Why is the shedding of blood essential to the sacrifice for sin?

16. What do Scriptures teach that the precious blood of Christ accomplishes?

17. What are some of the promises that God will answer prayer?

18. What are some of the conditions that relate to God's answer to prayer?

19. How can prayer be defined?
20. Explain how a check with two signatures illustrates prayer.
21. How does prayer change things even if the prayer is not answered?
22. How does the fact that Christ in His resurrection lives forever relate to His intercession for us?
23. How much of God's attention do we have moment by moment?
24. To what extent are we joining a prayer meeting already in session?
25. How do wrong motives hinder answers to prayer?
26. Is it possible to miss blessing because we do not ask for it?
27. In summarizing God's provision for the Christian and its availability, how are we to experience spiritual power in our life?

[12]

When Christ Comes for the Church

DURING THE LIFETIME OF CHRIST the disciples did not understand that some prophecies were to be fulfilled in relation to the first coming of Christ and others in relation to His second coming. It was not until Christ died, rose again, and ascended into heaven that it became clear to the disciples that He would not fulfill the prophecies relating to His second coming until He returned. Accordingly, When will Christ return? became a very important question.

Likewise, for the Christian who comes to understand that Christ died for him and rose again and who enters into the wonder of his salvation as he walks and has intimate fellowship with Him, it is only natural to long to see Christ face to face. The church is described in Scripture as a bride waiting for her husband (2 Cor. 11:2). Just as a bride looks forward eagerly to her coming marriage, when she will begin her life with the bridegroom, so a believer in Christ, even though he is thrilled with the fellowship he has with Christ now, looks forward to that fuller fellowship that will be his when he is in Christ's presence forever. This is why the hope of Christ's return is called a blessed or happy hope (Titus 2:13). The more one loves Christ and seeks to have more intimate fellowship with Him, the more he will be looking for the return of Christ for him.

The first coming of Christ fulfilled hundreds of prophecies in the Old Testament. As the Old Testament predicted, Christ was born in Bethlehem (Micah 5:2); He was both God and man (Isa. 7:14); He was born of a virgin (Matt. 1:23); He performed miracles (Isa. 35:5–6); He died on the cross for the sins of the whole world as predicted in the Old Testament as well as in the Gospels (Isa. 53:6; 1 Cor. 15:1–3); and He rose again the third day, predicted in Psalm 16:9–11, and frequently mentioned by Christ Himself (Matt. 16:4, 21; 17:22; 20:18–19; Mark 8:31; 9:31; 10:33–34; Luke 9:22; 18:31–33; John 10:15, 17–18).

The present age followed His life on earth, and Christ's discourse in John 13–17 outlined the major features of this age. The present age, however, will conclude with the return of Christ. All the church creeds that are orthodox include the idea that Christ is coming again as revealed in both the Old and New Testaments. Christ Himself spoke on this extensively in Matthew 24. In His second coming to the earth, He will set up His kingdom for a thousand years and reign on the throne of David (Luke 1:32–33; Rev. 20:4–6).

Not revealed in the Old Testament is the prediction of Christ that He would come and take His disciples to heaven. This was included in His Upper Room Discourse in John 14:3, where Christ said, "If I go and prepare a place for you, I will come back and take you to be with me that you also may be where I am." Though some people try to harmonize this with the doctrine of the Second Coming, it is actually a different event because here believers will be taken from earth to heaven, whereas in the Second Coming, Christ will come from heaven to earth to remain in the earth to set up His kingdom. The disciples did not understand this, and Christ did not explain it, as the disciples were in no condition to understand it. Actually, a number of tremendous events have to take place *after* Christ comes for His church but *before* His second coming, and this includes the rise of a world church, the formation of a world government led by a world dictator, and the regathering of Israel to her ancient land, a prophecy that is already being fulfilled. The period between Christ's coming for His church and His second coming to the earth is climaxed by a time of unparalleled trouble that will last for three-and-a-half years and will culminate in a gigantic world war that will be fought in the Holy Land. While this is still underway, Christ will come back to set up His earthly kingdom.

In the Scriptures, however, whenever Christ's coming *for* His saints is mentioned, it is always presented as an imminent event, that is, no events are predicted as preceding it. This is in contrast to His second coming to set up His kingdom. Many prophecies in both the Old and New Testaments must be fulfilled before His second coming can be realized.

The Church as a Major Purpose of God

To understand prophecy it is important to determine the different programs of God. These include the contrast between all who are saved and go to heaven and all who are lost and will be cast into the lake of fire.

Other distinctions arise in Scripture that may or may not be related to the question of salvation. One of these is God's plan for the world, or the Gentiles. This is revealed especially in Daniel 2, 7, and 8. There it is revealed that four great empires would emerge in history: Babylon, Medo-Persia, Greece, and Rome. Preceding these historically were Egypt and Assyria, which figured largely in the history of Israel before Babylon. In all, six world empires were described in history and prophecy.

The final world empire, or the seventh empire, will be the kingdom from heaven, which will come after the Second Coming (Dan. 7:13–14). From God's point of view, these seven empires embrace the significant history of the world.

Another major program of God is His plan for Israel. This began with Abraham, Isaac, and Jacob, and the twelve tribes descending from Jacob's twelve sons. Most of the Old Testament deals with Israel's program. Promised in the Old Testament is a triumphant and glorious future kingdom to be brought in by the Second Coming. Christ will restore Israel spiritually and politically in her promised land along with His worldwide government over the Gentiles.

Revealed in the New Testament but not in the Old Testament is God's purpose in the present age to form the church as the body of Christ consisting of both Jews and Gentiles to fulfill a purpose different from His purpose for the Gentiles or Israel. The church is especially designed to illustrate the grace of God (Eph. 2:4–10). This will be its function in time and eternity. As the program for Gentiles reveals God's sovereignty and infinite power, and as Israel reveals God's faithfulness, love, and righteousness, so the church is designed to illustrate the grace of God.

Much of the confusion in the interpretation of prophecy may be traced to confusion of God's plan for Israel and His plan for the church. At the Rapture, the program of God for the church ends its progress on earth and begins its program in heaven. By contrast, the program for Israel and the program for the Gentiles will continue on earth. To some extent all the programs converge in the millennial kingdom and the eternal state that follows.

Prophecies of the Rapture

Though Christ did not stop to explain to the disciples what He meant in John 14, as they were not prepared to understand, it was given to the apostle Paul many years later when writing his first letter to the Thessalonians to outline exactly what would be done at the Rapture. In 1 Thessalonians 4:16–17 Paul stated, "The Lord himself will come down from heaven, with a loud command, with the voice of the archangel and with the trumpet call of God, and the dead in Christ will rise first. After that, we who are still alive and are left will be caught up together with them in the clouds to meet the Lord in the air. And so we will be with the Lord forever."

As these verses show, Christ will come bodily from heaven, where He is now seated at the right hand of the Father, to the air above the earth. This event will also feature the voice of the archangel who will give a shout of triumph. The rapture of the church will be accomplished in spite of all that Satan has done to hinder the church and people coming to Christ, and together they will rise to meet the Lord in the air, being raptured or snatched up, and subsequently go to heaven.

According to 1 Thessalonians 4:14, when Jesus comes from heaven to the air above the earth, He will bring with Him the souls of Christians who have died, as these souls have been in His presence in heaven. Now He brings them back to the sphere of earth because He is going to resurrect their bodies and their souls will reenter their bodies forever. At the same time living Christians are changed, and both those resurrected and those on earth will receive bodies that are suited for heaven, patterned after the resurrection body of Christ.

As John 14:3 indicates, once they meet the Lord in the air, they will proceed in triumphal procession to heaven, to the Father's house, an event that will pave the way for great prophecies to be fulfilled on earth preceding His return to set up His kingdom.

In 1 Corinthians 15:51–58 more light is thrown upon the character of the change that will take place at that time. Paul points out in 1 Corinthians 15:50 that people in their natural bodies need to have a change before they can be with the Lord because our present bodies are sinful, they are subject to age and decay, and they are subject to death. A resurrection body should be without sin and without advancing age and without death. Accordingly, Paul writes in 1 Corinthians 15:51–53, "Listen, I tell you a mystery: We will not all sleep, but we will all be changed—in a flash, in the twinkling of an eye, at the last trumpet. For the trumpet will sound, the dead will be raised imperishable, and we will be changed. For the perishable must clothe itself with the imperishable, and the mortal with immortality."

The fact that those raised from the dead and those translated will have new bodies is confirmed by Ephesians 5:27, where it is revealed that Christ will "present her to himself as a radiant church, without stain or wrinkle or any other blemish, but holy and blameless." The same thought is given in Philippians 3:21, where it states that Christ "will transform our lowly bodies so that they will be like his glorious body."

The resurrection of saints who have died refers only to Christians who are saved in the present age and who are "in Christ" (1 Thess. 4:16). Apparently, those who died in the Old Testament and those who die in the coming period after the church is raptured will be raised at the time of Christ's second coming because this is inferred in Daniel 12:1–2 and Revelation 20:4. The wicked, however, are not raised until after the Millennium (Rev. 20:5–6, 12–13).

Contrast Between the Rapture and the Second Coming

Christ's coming for His church is often designated as the Rapture. This is based on the statement of 1 Thessalonians 4:17 where those who are resurrected, or translated, are "caught up together with them in the clouds to meet the Lord in the air." The idea of being "caught up" is embraced in the word *rapture*, or *snatched up*, and this is what will occur at the time of Christ's coming for His church.

The Rapture, however, stands in sharp contrast to what will occur at the Second Coming.

(1) Christ's coming at the Rapture is to take saints from the earth to the Father's house in heaven, in contrast to the Second Coming, when the saints will come from heaven to earth and remain in the sphere of earth throughout Christ's millennial kingdom.

(2) At the Rapture those who are "in Christ," believers during the present age, will be resurrected from the dead, and living Christians will be translated, in contrast to the Second Coming, when no one will be translated.

(3) At the Rapture only the church is caught up to heaven in contrast to the Second Coming, when Old Testament saints and tribulation saints will be resurrected but remain in the earth.

(4) The Rapture of the church will remove the church before the time of judgment preceding the Second Coming, in contrast to the Second Coming, when believers on earth

who are under persecution will be rescued by Christ but will remain in the earthly sphere.

(5) The Rapture is revealed in Scripture to be an imminent event, that is, there are no predicted events that precede the Rapture, in contrast to the Second Coming before which many important world-shaking prophecies must be fulfilled as seen in Revelation 6–18.

(6) The Rapture is a New Testament truth, whereas the doctrine of the second coming of Christ to the earth is revealed in both Testaments.

(7) The Rapture relates to those who are saved with no judgments on earth, in contrast to the Second Coming, which will deal with both saved and unsaved.

(8) Before and after the Rapture Satan will still be active, but after the Rapture Satan will be allowed even greater activity (2 Thess. 2:3–10; Rev. 12:12). At the Second Coming, however, Satan will be bound for a thousand years (Rev. 20:1–3).

(9) The purpose of the Rapture is to take saints from earth to heaven, in contrast to the Second Coming, which involves resurrection of the Old Testament saints and the tribulation saints who remain on earth. Later, at the Second Coming those raptured earlier will join those still living in the world who will enter the millennial kingdom.

(10) At the Rapture there is no judgment of the world, whereas Matthew 25:31–46 indicates that Gentiles will be judged in regard to entering the millennial kingdom. Also, Jews will experience a similar judgment (Ezek. 20:33–38).

(11) If all the saints had been raptured at the time of the Second Coming and met Christ in the air, the judgment of the Gentiles in Matthew 25:31–46 would be unnecessary, because there would have already been a separation of the saints from those not saved while Christ was coming from

heaven to earth (1 Thess. 4:16–17). The fact that this judgment takes place after the Second Coming, when they are still intermingled, is proof that the Rapture did not take place as a part of the Second Coming.

(12) In Scripture the Rapture relates to the church, both living and dead, in contrast to the Second Coming, which relates primarily to Israel and the Gentiles as such.

(13) The Rapture is a blessed hope, a happy expectation, which could take place at any time, in contrast to the Second Coming, which can be realized only after the Great Tribulation when the majority of the earth's population will have perished in one disaster or another.

(14) The Rapture is a comforting hope (John 14:1–3; 1 Thess. 4:18), in contrast to the Second Coming, where the hope of survival is realized only by a few.

(15) The world probably will not see Christ at the time of the Rapture as the church will be taken out of the world instantly, in contrast to the Second Coming, which is a majestic procession of the saints and angels from heaven to earth which will take many hours and the whole earth will see.

Practical Aspects of the Rapture

God intended that the revelation of the Rapture be a blessing. In John 14 it was part of the reassurance that Christ gave His disciples, who were struggling with His predicted death on the cross. In 1 Thessalonians 4:18 the Rapture is presented as an encouraging, or comforting, hope. At the Rapture, of course, Christians will see their loved ones who have died and preceded them to heaven. It will also end their earthly problems, and they will be forever with the Lord. Because this event is imminent, it is all the more real and precious.

The promise of the coming of the Lord is also a purifying hope, because Christians realize that after the Lord comes they will be judged at the judgment seat of Christ. Scripture makes it very clear that every human being will be judged before entering the life after this, but these judgments do not occur at the same time. This is an important factor for Christians to consider in relation to the Rapture, because the judgment of every Christian at the judgment seat of Christ immediately follows the Rapture.

The central truth of the judgment seat of Christ is stated in 2 Corinthians 5:10, "For we must all appear before the judgment seat of Christ, that each one may receive what is due him for the things done while in the body, whether good or bad." As this text makes clear, this is a judgment for Christians only, as the issue of salvation was already settled by the fact of their rapture to heaven.

This judgment is not concerned with the sins of Christians, as the words "good or bad" are words relating to value, not morality. The question is whether a Christian's life included things of eternal value in God's sight.

When a person becomes a Christian he is "justified through faith" (Rom. 5:1). This means he is declared righteous. To be declared righteous is more than being forgiven, as forgiveness is subtracting or wiping away our sins, while being declared righteous is the declaration that we possess the quality of righteousness.

This can be illustrated in the function of a checking account. If one has a checking account and overdraws his account, the bank may honor the check but notify the depositor that he is overdrawn. If anyone deposited the amount of the overdraft in the account, it would bring the account back to zero and the depositor would be forgiven. However, if someone deposited a large amount of money in the account, it would not only wipe out the deficit but add credit to the account. The believer is in a position of having a credit. Not only are his sins forgiven but he has credited to him the righteousness of Christ because God sees him in the perfections of the person and work of His Son.

The basis for justification is that a believer was baptized by the Holy Spirit and placed "in Christ" (Eph. 1:4–12) when he believed, so that God from then on views his *position* as "in Christ." In this position, the believer is "a new creation" (2 Cor. 5:17). He is seen in the moral perfection of the Person and the work of Christ. Accordingly, Paul argues in Romans 8:31–34, "What, then, shall we say in response to this? If God is for us, who can be against us? He who did not spare his own Son, but gave him up for us all—how will he not also, along with him, graciously give us all things? Who will bring any charge against those whom God has chosen? It is God who justifies. Who is he that condemns? Christ Jesus, who died—more than that, who was raised to life—is at the right hand of God and is also interceding for us."

Though a believer is perfect in his position, his *state* is far less than perfect, and he is subject to experiential sanctification as he becomes more and more in conformity to perfection in Christ. The believer must also avail himself of the promise of forgiveness upon confession to have unhindered fellowship (1 John 1:9). When the believer is raptured, however, he achieves immediate perfection in the spiritual state conforming to his perfection position in Christ. Hence, the judgment seat of Christ does not deal with sins but with the service of a believer while on earth.

Paul uses three illustrations to teach this doctrine. In 1 Corinthians 3:10–15 he compares our life to a building to be tested by fire:

By the grace God has given me, I laid a foundation as an expert builder, and someone else is building on it. But each one should be careful how he builds. For no one can lay any foundation other than the one already laid, which is Jesus Christ. If any man builds on this foundation using gold, silver, costly stones, wood, hay or straw, his work will be shown for what it is, because the Day will bring it to light. It will be revealed with fire, and the fire will test the quality of each man's work. If what he has built survives, he will receive his reward. If it is burned up, he will suffer loss; he himself will be saved, but only as one escaping through the flames.

The building is built on a foundation that is supplied—Jesus Christ, our salvation. The materials of the building, though not explained, illustrate various values in life: (1) gold refers to what is done to the glory of God; (2) silver represents the metal of redemption and speaks of soul winning; (3) precious stones represent any work reflecting the glory of God that has eternal value.

In contrast, the wood, hay, or straw represent values not eternal: (1) wood represents things of value by the world's standard, but not eternal; (2) hay represents food for animals but not eternal in value; (3) straw represents a thing that has little value in this life and no worth in eternity. The fire does not destroy the gold, silver, and precious stones, but the wood, hay, and straw are reduced to ashes. The challenge to a Christian is to build into his life that which corresponds to gold, silver, and precious stones.

In a second illustration in 1 Corinthians 9:24–27 Paul compares this life to a race:

Do you not know that in a race all the runners run, but only one gets the prize? Run in such a way as to get the prize. Everyone who competes in the games goes into strict training. They do it to get a crown that will not last; but we do it to get a crown that will last forever. Therefore I do not run like a man running aimlessly; I do not fight like a man beating the air. No, I beat my body and make it my slave so that after I have preached to others, I myself will not be disqualified for the prize.

When in college athletics, I had occasion to observe a fellow student who was an expert runner. Almost always when he ran a race he would win. It was a thrill to see him line up at the start, get on his mark, and when the starter said "go," instantly start the race. Before long he would be leading the others. There were certain things I noticed he never did as a runner. He did not wear his top coat or heavy clothing but wore light clothing that would not hinder movement. When the starter said "go," he did not ask whether the starter meant him, but he would immediately start the race. As he ran, he would never look back to see the other runners, because this would cause him to lose stride, and he might lose the race. Also, he never stopped to pick flowers along the way. While picking flowers was not a crime, he would lose the race if he did this. Furthermore, he never waved at the grandstand as he ran by, though his friends were there. He concentrated on running the race, and everything else was put aside to win the prize.

The way my friend ran the race can teach us many lessons that apply to the Christian life. How we need to leave aside everything that would hinder our running the race! When the Lord says "go," we should go instantly. We should give the race all the strength we have. We should not be diverted into things that may be good but may not be the will of God for us. We should not be concerned about whether people notice what we are doing, for God is our judge and He will reward. Life is certainly like a race. As we run the race, we should run to win and fulfill God's will for our lives.

Races were common in Corinth. The victor was given a crown of laurel leaves, which soon decayed. Paul urged Christians to qualify for a crown that would not decay, given at the judgment seat of Christ.

Paul offers another illustration in Romans 14:10–12: "Why do you judge your brother? Or why do you look down on your brother? For we will all stand before God's judgment seat. It is written: ' "As surely as I live," says the Lord, "every knee will bow before me; every tongue will confess to God." ' So then, each of us will give an account of himself to God."

The figure is that of a steward or trustee who has committed unto him something that actually belongs to another. As a boy I used to love to go with my father to our little bank with its row of cashiers behind the iron grating. I was always impressed by the amount of money they had in their booths. It was not until I became older that I realized that the money did not belong to them but belonged to the bank. They were stewards or trustees and had to report the day's transactions each evening.

This truth was reinforced when I saw one of our Dallas Seminary students serving as a cashier. I asked him later how it worked. He said that at the beginning of the day he had checked out to him the amount of money he would need for the transactions of the day. All day money would come in and go out. At the end of the day, however, he had to account for every penny, as none of the money belonged to him.

Paul asked the question, "What do you have that you did not receive?" (1 Cor. 4:7). The more we receive the greater is our responsibility. Christians are saved and given spiritual gifts by God as a solemn trust, that they be used wisely. Christians should not attempt to judge others in regard to reward, for each will have to give account to God and to no one else.

This figure is the great leveler of human attainment. Judgment is on the basis of faithful use of gifts, not necessarily how successful an individual may be. Every Christian has an equal opportunity for reward, because those with few gifts must account only for what God gave them. Those with many gifts actually have the greater difficulty of using all that God has given them. Many an obscure Christian will be rewarded more than those who had many gifts. Therefore, comparison of one Christian's life to another's is unwise.

These truths will come into focus, especially at the time of the Rapture. The fact that the Rapture is an imminent event that could occur at any time teaches us the importance of making the most of our present opportunities, whether in the form of witness, stewardship, or holy living. Paul's exhortation in 1 Corinthians 15:58 is most appropriate with regard to the Rapture when he says, "Stand firm. Let nothing move you. Always give yourselves fully to the work of the Lord, because you know that your labor in the Lord is not in vain."

Questions

1. Was it natural for the disciples to long to see Christ in His return to the earth?
2. How does a bride awaiting marriage illustrate the

church waiting for the coming of Christ?

3. What were some of the important prophecies that the Old Testament predicted that were fulfilled in Christ's life on earth?

4. Why is the Upper Room Discourse, John 13–17, important for Christians today?

5. How did Christ describe His second coming in Matthew 24:23–27?

6. What Scriptures indicate that at the second coming of Christ He will begin a kingdom for a thousand years on earth and will reign on the throne of David?

7. What new truth was introduced by Christ in John 14?

8. Why is this a different coming than His second coming to set up His kingdom?

9. What are some of the tremendous events that will precede His second coming to set up His kingdom?

10. What characterizes the last three-and-a-half years preceding the Second Coming?

11. What do you gather from the fact that the Rapture as presented in Scripture is always considered an imminent event, that is, no preceding events are mentioned?

12. What major division of the human race is involved in God's purpose and plan?

13. What was the broad outline of God's plan for the Gentile world as revealed in the Old Testament and especially in Daniel?

14. What were the six world empires anticipated in the Old Testament?

15. What will characterize the seventh kingdom, which will follow the Roman Empire?

16. What is the broad outline of God's plan and purpose for Israel? How is this related to the Second Coming?

17. What is God's present purpose for the church? What does it reveal about the character of God?
18. What did Paul reveal in 1 Thessalonians 4:16–17 concerning the Rapture?
19. Why will Christ bring with Him the souls of Christians who have died?
20. What will be the effect of the Rapture on the bodies of Christians who have died and those who are living?
21. What are some of the major things wrong with our present body that need to be corrected before we can go to heaven?
22. Describe the beauty of the church as anticipated in Ephesians 5:27.
23. Who will be included in the rapture of the church?
24. When will other people who are saved be raised from the dead?
25. When will the wicked be raised from the dead?
26. What are some of the major contrasts between the Rapture and the Second Coming?
27. Why do these differences reinforce the fact that the Rapture is a different event than the Second Coming?
28. What are some of the practical aspects of the Rapture?
29. Why is the Rapture a comforting hope?
30. Why is the Rapture a purifying hope?
31. What is the nature of the judgment seat of Christ?
32. Why is the judgment seat of Christ not concerned with the matter of salvation?
33. What is meant by justification?
34. Though a believer is justified, how do you explain the work of sanctification?
35. When will a believer's state be as perfect as his position?
36. How does a building and its materials illustrate the

judgment seat of Christ? What does this teach about the quality of our life now, anticipating the coming of Christ?

37. What is taught by the illustration of running a race in respect to the judgment seat of Christ?

38. What are some of the things a runner does not do who wants to win the race?

39. In what respects is the judgment seat of Christ an illustration of stewardship or being a trustee?

40. How does the illustration of stewardship bring equality to Christians regardless of their ability? In what way does this give all believers an equal opportunity to obtain God's rewards?

41. What is Paul's final exhortation regarding the Rapture in 1 Corinthians 15:58?

[13]

Major Events Preceding the Second Coming of Christ

THE SECOND COMING OF CHRIST is preceded by a number of world-shaking events that must occur before Christ can return. This is in contrast to the rapture of the church, which is always presented in Scripture as an imminent event. The Second Coming, however, is a climax of what God is doing with the world to prepare it for Christ's millennial kingdom. Many detailed prophecies relate to this period, and understanding this helps one to analyze current world affairs as shaping up in preparation for these events.

The Revival of the Roman Empire

In Daniel's presentation of the four great empires in chapter 7, the fourth empire, though not named, is clearly to be identified with the Roman government. In the revelation of Daniel 7, the prophet sees four great beasts, the first being a lion, representing Babylon, the second a bear, representing Medo-Persia, and the third a leopard, representing the empire of Alexander. The student of Daniel's prophecies does not have to guess at this because

Daniel names the second and third empires as that of Medo-Persia and Greece (Daniel 8:20–21). The fourth beast, which follows the Grecian empire, however, is not named but is described as "terrifying and frightening and very powerful. It had large iron teeth; it crushed and devoured its victims and trampled underfoot whatever was left. It was different from all the former beasts, and it had ten horns" (Dan. 7:7). The description here of the fourth empire fits accurately the Roman Empire from God's point of view.

The Roman legion conquered country after country and carried off able-bodied men as slaves and enforced their rule by leaving contingents of soldiers in each country. It literally "devoured its victims and trampled underfoot" each country. In the explanation given to Daniel concerning the four beasts and the ten kingdoms, he was told: "The fourth beast is a fourth kingdom that will appear on earth. It will be different from all the other kingdoms and will devour the whole earth, trampling it down and crushing it. The ten horns are ten kings who will come from this kingdom" (Dan. 7:23–24). The prophecies of the four empires have already been fulfilled in history except that the Roman Empire has never developed into a ten-nation kingdom. Accordingly, many believe that this is a future situation that will take place after the Rapture of the church.

Many prophecies of the Old Testament that deal with the end of the age leap from the first coming of Christ to the second coming of Christ without taking into account the present age. This is true of the feet of the image in Daniel 2, and it is also true of the prophecy concerning the fourth kingdom, which today seemingly has disappeared, but in Scripture will be revived in the ten-nation form preceding the second coming of Christ. As the fourth kingdom is finally terminated by Jesus Christ's coming from heaven (Dan. 7:13–14), it becomes clear that this form of the kingdom will emerge before the second coming of Christ.

The Emergence of Antichrist

In addition to explaining that the empire will consist of ten kingdoms, Daniel was told that there will be an eleventh horn, an individual who will conquer them all. This is stated in Daniel 7:8, "While I was thinking about the horns, there before me was another horn, a little one, which came up among them; and three of the first horns were uprooted before it. This horn had eyes like the eyes of a man and a mouth that spoke boastfully." This eleventh horn, obviously, is another king distinct from the ten kings mentioned earlier. At Daniel's request, explanation was given to him about it in Daniel 7:24, "After them another king will arise, different from the earlier ones; he will subdue three kings." As it is also stated in 7:23, he will eventually conquer the entire world, and it seems clear that he gains control of all these ten kingdoms before he rises to become a world dictator.

In Revelation 13:1–10 another prophetic vision was given concerning this fourth beast. Revelation 13:1 states that it has ten horns and ten crowns. In the final empire, the beast gathers in all of the preceding empires pictured as a lion, a bear, and a leopard. John writes, "The beast I saw resembled a leopard, but had feet like those of a bear and a mouth like that of a lion" (Rev. 13:2). From Daniel 7 and Revelation 13 it may be concluded that the Bible speaks of a future world empire that will be a revival of the Roman Empire that was in existence when Christ was on earth. The extent of the power of this world empire is given in Revelation 13:5–7:

The beast was given a mouth to utter proud words and blasphemies and to exercise his authority for forty-two months. He opened his mouth to blaspheme God, and to slander his name and his dwelling place and those who live in heaven. He was given power to make war against the saints and to conquer them. And he was given authority over every tribe, people, language and nation.

According to the book of Revelation, this ruler will head the world government for forty-two months. This forty-two month period is the last three-and-a-half years prior to the second coming of Christ. In that period there will be a time of unprecedented trouble. This is described in Daniel 12:1, "There will be a time of distress such as has not happened from the beginning of nations until then. But at that time your people—everyone whose name is found written in the book—will be delivered."

Christ also spoke of this time of trouble preceding His second coming when He told some of the disciples, "For then there will be great distress, unequaled from the beginning of the world until now—and never to be equaled again. If those days had not been cut short, no one would survive, but for the sake of the elect those days will be shortened" (Matt. 24:21–22). In Matt. 24:29–30 Christ goes on to explain to His disciples that His second coming will bring this time of trouble to a close:

Immediately after the distress of those days 'the sun will be darkened, and the moon will not give its light; the stars will fall from the sky, and the heavenly bodies will be shaken.' At that time the sign of the Son of Man will appear in the sky, and all the nations of the earth will mourn. They will see the Son of Man coming on the clouds of the sky, with power and great glory.

The Covenant with Israel

Christ will deal with the world of the Gentiles pictured in the ten-nation group and the world empire that follows, according to Daniel, in the seven-year period leading up to His second coming. This is part of the "seventy times seven" (490) years of God's dealing with the people of Israel (Dan. 9:24–27), beginning with the restoration of the city of Jerusalem in 444 B.C.

These 490 years, however, are divided into three periods, with the first two consecutive, but the last seven years will be separated from the preceding period by the present age that intervenes, during which God is calling out His church. Once the rapture of the church takes place, however, it will be possible for God to bring about the fulfillment of the last seven years described in Daniel 9:27, "He [the ruler who will come, v. 26] will confirm a covenant with many for one 'seven.' In the middle of the 'seven' he will put an end to sacrifice and offering." The last seven years preceding the Second Coming begin when the covenant is made, probably shortly after the Rapture.

Daniel 9:27 describes the final seven years leading up to the second coming of Christ and divides it into two periods, the first being the three-and-a-half years during which the covenant is observed and the second being the three-and-a-half years when the covenant is broken, resulting in the termination of Jewish sacrifices in their temple. The Jews will make this seven-year covenant with the ruler over the ten kingdoms who later becomes the world dictator. Though the term *Antichrist* is never applied directly to this world ruler, he will be the ultimate fulfillment of predictions of the Antichrist (1 John 2:18, 22; 4:3; 2 John 7).

Antichrist is anyone who opposes Christ or who claims to be a substitute for Christ. The apostle John declared that *the* Antichrist is coming, but that there are many antichrists: "Dear children, this is the last hour; and as you have heard that the antichrist is coming, even now many antichrists have come" (1 John 2:18). John further defines an antichrist, "Who is the liar? It is the man who denies that Jesus is the Christ. Such a man is the antichrist—he denies the Father and the Son" (1 John 2:22). John further describes an antichrist as one who denies that Christ came in the flesh as God in 1 John 4:3, "but every spirit that does not acknowledge Jesus is not from God. This is the spirit of the antichrist, which you have heard is coming and even now is already in the world." The same explanation is given in 2 John 7. The future world ruler who governs ten nations and later becomes dictator over the whole world is *the* Antichrist because he is against Christ and is a substitute for Christ, as the prefix "anti" means.

Three Periods Between the Rapture and the Second Coming

In a study of all the passages that relate to the end time, it becomes clear that there are three major time periods between the Rapture and the Second Coming. The first is the period of preparation, a relatively short period, in which the ten-nation kingdom emerges. Its leader rises to conquer first three and then all ten kingdoms. When this leader becomes powerful, because of his backing of the ten kingdoms, he is able to make the covenant with Israel for seven years described in Daniel 9:27. This introduces the second period of time, which covers the first half of the seven years mentioned in the covenant. In the middle of the seven years, however, a dramatic change takes place, and the ruler of the ten kingdoms becomes a world dictator, apparently without a war. This sets the stage for the third period, the last three-and-a-half years leading up to the second coming of Christ. Accordingly, there is first a period of preparation leading up to the seven-year period. Then there will be three-and-a-half years of peace, the second period, and this will be followed by the third of great trouble and tribulation. The third period will be followed immediately by the Second Coming.

The War with the Soviet Union

In Ezekiel 38–39 a strange war is predicted in which a great nation to the north of Israel, a reference to the Soviet Union (Ezek. 36:15; 38:6, 15; 39:2), will be joined by a number of other nations in a sneak attack upon Israel at a time when Israel is at peace (Ezek. 38:11). Though a number of explanations have been given of the prophecy, it seems that this Soviet invasion will come during the first three-and-a-half years leading up to the second coming of Christ. This would correspond to the time of peace described in Ezekiel 38 (see 1 Thess. 5:3). This war turns out to be a disaster for the Soviet Union and her other allies (Ezek. 39:3–6, 11–20) as they will be annihilated.

The destruction of the invaders will change the world situation, which apparently then will be much like it is now, with the Soviet Union and her allies opposed to the rest of the world. With the Soviet Union out of the way as a military power because of the destruction of her army, it will be possible for the ruler of the ten kingdoms to declare himself a world dictator, and apparently, there will be no power great enough to oppose him, and a world empire will be born overnight. At the beginning of his world empire the world will ask the question, "Who is like the beast? Who can make war against him?" (Rev. 13:4). And the answer is that no one will be strong enough to deny the ruler of the ten kingdoms the place of a dictatorship over the entire world.

When this takes place and the world empire suddenly emerges, the Middle East ruler will break his covenant with Israel and become her persecutor instead of her protector, and the final three-and-a-half years leading up to the second coming of Christ will be a time of trouble for Israel and for the entire world. The world ruler of the end time will not only claim political rule over all nations but will also claim to be God (Rev. 13:8).

According to Daniel 11:37, the world ruler "will show no regard for the gods of his fathers or for the one desired by women, nor will he regard any god, but will exalt himself above them all." According to Daniel 11:38, he will worship only the power to make war and gain victory, and he will be engaged in warfare toward the end of that last three-and-a-half years.

The Great Tribulation: Armageddon

As indicated in the breaking of the covenant with Israel, the future world ruler will bring on a terrible time of persecution by the government and judgment of God upon the world. This time of trouble is described graphically in Revelation 6–18. This period will include disasters from God as well as persecution of all those who will not recognize the world ruler as deity.

In his vision recorded in Revelation 6, John is

introduced to a scroll with seven seals affixed to the side. As the scroll is unrolled, each seal is broken, signaling a great event on the earth. Some of these are great catastrophies. Seal one refers to the world empire that is brought out at the beginning of the three-and-a-half years. This is indicated by the bow without an arrow (Rev. 6:2), the formation of the world empire without a fight.

Seals two and three refer to warfare and starvation, which will affect many. The fourth seal reveals that one-fourth of the earth's population will be destroyed, certainly a time of the wrath of God. The fifth seal recognizes that the world ruler will put to death those who do not recognize him as deity, and they are seen in heaven waiting for the time when the world ruler will be judged. In this period, according to the sixth seal, great disturbances will take place in the earth, with the sun darkened, the moon turning blood red, and stars of heaven falling to earth. There will also be a great earthquake, with every mountain and island removed from its place (Rev. 6:12–14).

Out of the seventh seal will come a second series of sevens called trumpets. As each trumpet is sounded, it signals another tremendous judgment on earth, usually extending to one-third of the earth's area (Rev. 9:7–12), and one-third of the earth's population will be destroyed (Rev. 9:15). Again, there will be great disturbances in nature, and eventually war.

Out of the seventh trumpet will come a third series of sevens called vials, or bowls, of the wrath of God. Each of these introduces another tremendous judgment on earth, usually extending to the entire earth. The first bowl judgment poured out will cause painful sores on people who have been worshiping the world ruler and the idol of him that was set up in the temple (Rev. 16:1–2). The second bowl pictures judgment on the sea so that every living creature in it dies (Rev. 16:3). The third bowl of the wrath of God will corrupt the springs of water, and they will become blood (Rev. 16:4). The fourth bowl will disturb the ordinary course of the sun, and people will be scorched because of the intense heat (Rev. 16:8). The fifth bowl results in the earth's being plunged into darkness, because the heavens will be so disturbed that they do not give their normal light (Rev. 16:10). The sixth bowl will dry up the river Euphrates, which will make it possible for a great army from the East to approach the Holy Land and join in the final great war that is described taking place there. The final bowl of wrath will consist of a great earthquake that destroys the cities of the world, causing mountains and islands to disappear, and apparently the topography of the entire earth will be changed (Rev. 16:17–21).

During the three-and-a-half years of the Great Tribulation, God protected 144,000 Israelites, 12,000 in each tribe, as described in Revelation 7. They were able to go through the Great Tribulation unscathed and will be on Mount Zion at the end of the Great Tribulation (Rev. 14:1). By contrast, however, Revelation 7:9–17 pictures a great multitude in heaven consisting of those who have been martyred because they would not worship the world ruler and his claim for deity. By putting all these tremendous disasters of the end time together, we are introduced to a world scene where most of the world's population has been destroyed prior to the second coming of Christ, and many of those who did turn to Christ in that day have become martyrs. In the Great Tribulation the final form of anti-God religion will consist of the atheistic worship of the world ruler and a denial of the true God. When Christ returns, He will judge the wickedness of the earth, rescue those still living in the earth who are saved and bring them into the millennial kingdom, and bring judgment of physical death on all the others (Matt. 24:30–31; 25:31–45).

Questions

1. According to Scripture, what events precede the Rapture?
2. By contrast, what events precede the second coming of Christ?
3. What are the four great world empires described by Daniel?
4. How does the fourth empire resemble the Roman Empire?
5. What is the evidence that there will be a future revival of the Roman Empire in the form of a ten-nation kingdom?
6. Who does the eleventh horn of Daniel 7 represent?
7. How does the prophecy of the eleventh horn support the idea that the ten-nation kingdom is still ahead?
8. What does Revelation 13 add concerning the fourth empire?
9. What do we learn of the future world ruler in Revelation 13?
10. How long will be the period of his world rule?
11. How does the period of his world rule relate to the seven years preceding the Second Coming?
12. What does Revelation 13 teach concerning the coming Great Tribulation?
13. What did Christ have to say about the Great Tribulation?
14. What will climax the Great Tribulation?
15. Describe the last seven years leading up to the Second Coming in relation to Israel's covenant. How does

the forming of the covenant indicate the beginning of the seven years?

16. When will this covenant with Israel take place in relation to the Rapture?

17. What three time periods are found in the period between the Rapture and the Second Coming? And what occurs in each?

18. What is meant by *antichrist*? To what extent does it refer to a definite person of the future?

19. What scriptural evidence is there that there will be a war between the Soviet Union and Israel in the end time?

20. When will the war with Israel probably occur in relation to the last seven years leading up to the Second Coming?

21. What is the outcome of the war in relation to the Soviet Union and her allies?

22. How does this change the world situation and the position of the ruler of the ten kingdoms?

23. What are some of the things that occur at the time the world ruler takes power?

24. How would you describe the future world ruler?

25. How would you define the Great Tribulation?

26. What do the first six seals on the scroll represent?

27. What emerges from the seventh seal when it is broken?

28. What characterizes the trumpet judgments and what is their extent?

29. What comes out of the seventh trumpet?

30. How do the judgments relating to the bowls of the wrath of God compare to the trumpet judgments?

31. In what respect are the trumpet judgments similar to the judgments of the bowls of the wrath of God? And in what respects are they different?

32. What is the significance of the sixth bowl of the wrath of God?

33. How does the sixth bowl relate to the final great world war?

34. What is the result of the seventh bowl being poured out on the earth?

35. How does the 144,000 of Israel reflect God's keeping power even in the midst of the Great Tribulation? In contrast to those who are protected, what is predicted about many others, both Jews and Gentiles, who come to Christ in that period?

36. In general, describe the world scene at the time of the second coming of Christ.

[14]

The Second Coming of Christ and the Millennial Kingdom

The Second Coming of Christ in the Old Testament

THE SECOND COMING OF CHRIST is a major doctrine of both the Old and New Testaments, and all orthodox creeds include the fact of His second coming as a part of essential doctrine. The Psalms, though mostly devotional, contain a number of references to Christ's second coming. Early in Psalm 2 the writer says that the Lord scoffs at those who rebel against Him. The Psalm states:

Then he rebukes them in his anger and terrifies them in his wrath, saying, "I have installed my King on Zion, my holy hill." I will proclaim the decree of the LORD: He said to me, "You are my Son; today I have become your Father. Ask of me, and I will make the nations your inheritance, the ends of the earth your possession. You will rule them with an iron scepter; you will dash them to pieces like pottery" (Ps. 2:5–9).

The trilogy of Psalm 22, 23, and 24 gives a panoramic view of Christ. Psalm 22 speaks of His work as the Good Shepherd dying on the cross for our sins (John 10:11). Psalm 23 speaks of His present care for His own as the Great Shepherd (Heb. 13:20), interceding for them in heaven. Psalm 24 describes Christ as the King of Glory, the Chief Shepherd (1 Peter 5:4), who will enter the gates of Jerusalem.

Another major revelation is given in Psalm 72, revealing Christ's reign over the whole earth. After describing how He will judge the people, defend the afflicted, and deliver the righteous, the psalm continues:

> In his days the righteous will flourish; prosperity will abound till the moon is no more. He will rule from sea to sea and from the River to the ends of the earth. The desert tribes will bow before him and his enemies will lick the dust. The kings of Tarshish and of distant shores will bring tribute to him; the kings of Sheba and Seba will present him gifts. All kings will bow down to him and all nations will serve him (Ps. 72:7–11).

The Psalm concludes by stating that all nations will be blessed through Him and that the whole earth will be filled with His glory (Ps. 72:17–19).

Another major passage dealing with Christ in His second coming is found in Isaiah 11, where the righteous reign of Christ and the blessings of the millennial kingdom are revealed.

Daniel 7:13–14 states that the Second Coming marks the termination of the times of the Gentiles and the beginning of the reign of God's kingdom on earth:

> In my vision at night I looked, and there before me was one like a son of man, coming with the clouds of heaven. He approached the Ancient of Days and was

led into his presence. He was given authority, glory
and sovereign power; all peoples, nations and men
of every language worshiped him. His dominion is
an everlasting dominion that will not pass away, and
his kingdom is one that will never be destroyed.

This passage, as all others on the second coming of Christ,
makes clear that it refers to an event not yet fulfilled that
will consummate the plan of God for the ages.

Zechariah 2:10–11 also anticipates the coming of the
Lord and His residence in the earth, " 'Shout and be glad, O
Daughter of Zion. For I am coming, and I will live among
you,' declares the LORD. 'Many nations will be joined with
the LORD in that day and will become my people. I will live
among you and you will know that the LORD Almighty has
sent me to you.' " In that future day Scripture declares that
Christ will claim the Holy Land as His own. Zechariah
says, "The LORD will inherit Judah as his portion in the holy
land and will again choose Jerusalem" (Zech. 2:12).

A dramatic description of the second coming of Christ
is recorded in Zechariah 14, which describes an attack
upon Jerusalem. Zechariah states, "Then the LORD will go
out and fight against those nations, as he fights in the day
of battle. On that day his feet will stand on the Mount of
Olives, east of Jerusalem, and the Mount of Olives will be
split in two from east to west, forming a great valley, with
half of the mountain moving north and half moving south"
(Zech. 14:3–4). This prophecy makes clear that Christ has
not come in His second coming because the Mount of
Olives is still intact, awaiting the coming of Christ.

The Second Coming of Christ in the New Testament

In the New Testament, in addition to prophecies
concerning the Second Coming, the rapture of the church is

revealed for the first time. The rapture of the church is the occasion when Christ will come to take the church, living and dead, out of the earth to heaven. It is an event entirely different from the Second Coming, as the two comings are described.

About twenty passages deal with the subject of the Second Coming in the New Testament. They serve to emphasize that this is a major doctrine of Scripture (Matt. 19:28; 23:39; 24:3–25:46; Mark 13:24–37; Luke 12:35–48; 17:22–37; 18:8; 21:25–28; Acts 1:10–11; 15:16–18; Rom. 11:25–27; 1 Cor. 11:26; 2 Thess. 1:7–10; 2 Peter 3:3–4; Jude 14–15; Rev. 1:7–8; 2:25–28; 16:15; 19:11–21; 22:20).

Though liberal interpreters attempt to find some fulfillment of the second coming of Christ in present human experience, all conservative interpreters describe the Second Coming as a future major divine event fulfilling the revelation in Revelation 19:11–15. Also, there is general agreement that Christ will come personally and bodily in a return to the earth, which was prophesied in Acts 1:9–10. His return will be similar to His ascension in that He will return bodily, and it will be gradual and visible, with clouds as the angels prophesied when they said, "This same Jesus, who has been taken from you into heaven, will come back in the same way you have seen him go into heaven" (Acts 1:11). Some interpreters have attempted to incorporate the rapture of the church as a part of the Second Coming. A careful study of Revelation 19–20 reveals no textual support for a rapture in that sequence of events. The revelation of Christ at His second coming is painted graphically in Revelation 19:11–16:

> I saw heaven standing open and there before me was
> a white horse, whose rider is called Faithful and
> True. With justice he judges and makes war. His

eyes are like blazing fire, and on his head are many crowns. He has a name written on him that no one knows but he himself. He is dressed in a robe dipped in blood, and his name is the Word of God. The armies of heaven were following him, riding on white horses and dressed in fine linen, white and clean. Out of his mouth comes a sharp sword with which to strike down the nations. "He will rule them with an iron scepter." He treads the winepress of the fury of the wrath of God Almighty. On his robe and on his thigh he has this name written:

KING OF KINGS AND LORD OF LORDS.

There is no similarity whatever between this and His coming at the Rapture as brought out previously. At the Rapture there is no statement of anyone accompanying Him; there is no record that He ever judges the earth or that His purpose is to end the times of the Gentiles. In Revelation the second coming of Christ is pictured in contrast to His first coming. In His first coming He came quietly to live a life on earth; in His second coming He comes in His glory accompanied by the hosts of heaven. At the Second Coming there is no "catching up" of the church and taking it out of the world as is true of the Rapture. In the Second Coming the saints and angels will accompany Christ in His return and will remain in the earthly sphere to share in the millennial reign that follows. At His second coming Christ will destroy the armies of the world that were gathered to conquer the Holy Land. It is a terrible picture of divine judgment upon a wicked world that rejected Christ. The world leader described as the beast and the false prophet associated with him will be cast alive into the fiery lake of burning sulfur (Rev. 19:20).

Immediately after Christ returns and judges those who wickedly oppose Him, Satan will be rendered inactive for the first time, as Revelation 20:1–3 states:

I saw an angel coming down out of heaven, having the key to the Abyss and holding in his hand a great chain. He seized the dragon, that ancient serpent, who is the devil, or Satan, and bound him for a thousand years. He threw him into the Abyss, and locked and sealed it over him, to keep him from deceiving the nations anymore until the thousand years were ended. After that, he must be set free for a short time.

Distinction must be made in the interpretation of this passage between what John saw and what he was told. He saw what appeared to be Satan, described here also as the dragon, the serpent, and the devil. John saw him thrown into the abyss and saw the abyss locked and sealed, but he could not understand why unless he was told. God had to reveal that Satan would be bound for a thousand years and that he would not be able to deceive the nations in that thousand-year period. It also was revealed that at the end of the thousand years he would be set free for a short time (Rev. 20:3). The explanation should be understood as a literal interpretation.

This prophecy is certainly not fulfilled in the present age because the present age is not a thousand years and Satan is not bound in the present age. In fact, Scripture makes it clear, as in 1 Peter 5:8, that "your enemy the devil prowls around like a roaring lion looking for someone to devour." In the present age while Satan is limited by God, he is not bound or inactive and, as a matter of fact, is deceiving millions of people. As presented in Revelation 20, Satan's binding is the logical result of Christ's coming to judge the world, restore righteousness, and install His kingdom in which Satan will be inactive for the entire period of the thousand years.

In connection with the events following the second coming of Christ, John also saw the resurrection of those who had been martyred in the Great Tribulation during the three-and-a-half years preceding the Second Coming. John writes:

> I saw thrones on which were seated those who had been given authority to judge. And I saw the souls of those who had been beheaded because of their testimony for Jesus and because of the word of God. They had not worshiped the beast or his image and had not received his mark on their foreheads or their hands. They came to life and reigned with Christ a thousand years. (The rest of the dead did not come to life until the thousand years were ended.) This is the first resurrection. Blessed and holy are those who have part in the first resurrection. The second death has no power over them, but they will be priests of God and of Christ and will reign with him for a thousand years (Rev. 20:4–6).

It is significant that the resurrection of the tribulation saints, who died three-and-a-half years before in the three-and-a-half-year period leading up to the Second Coming, is accomplished in anticipation that they would in their resurrected life reign with Christ a thousand years. This introduces another important factor that bears on the Second Coming: it is premillennial, that is, it occurs before the thousand years. This is required by the resurrection of the martyred saints killed in the period just before His second coming. In fact, the coming of Christ results in the establishment of the millennial kingdom, which otherwise would not come about. In this passage the martyred dead of the tribulation are resurrected and subsequently reign for a thousand years with Christ.

The doctrine that there is one general resurrection of all people is also repudiated here because verse 5 states that the resurrection of the martyred dead is a selected resurrection and that the rest of the dead, that is, the wicked, will not be raised until after the thousand years. This is confirmed in the passage that follows, as described in Revelation 20:7–10, when the devil is released after the thousand years, begins to deceive the nations, and gains a large following, which surrounds Jerusalem and attempts to conquer it. Fire will come down from heaven and devour them, and Satan himself will be cast into the lake of burning sulfur where he will be tormented forever and ever. The resurrection of the wicked follows.

Judgments at the Time of the Second Coming of Christ

At the second coming of Christ there will be a series of judgments. Already mentioned is the judgment and reward of the martyred dead of the Great Tribulation. Also mentioned is the judgment of Satan, which causes him to be bound for a thousand years.

The Scriptures also speak of a general judgment of the nations, or the Gentiles (Matt. 25:31–46). This is a judgment of Gentiles living in the world at the time of the second coming of Christ who have survived the Great Tribulation. Those counted worthy are described as sheep, and they will be eligible to enter the millennial kingdom. Those who are counted unworthy, designated as goats, are put to death.

A similar judgment of the people of Israel is described in Ezekiel 20:33–38. Those counted worthy enter the millennial kingdom; those not counted worthy are put to death.

Not mentioned in Revelation is the resurrection and judgment of Old Testament saints as revealed in Daniel 12:2. Daniel writes, "Multitudes who sleep in the dust of the earth will awake: some to everlasting life, others to shame and everlasting contempt." The righteous are raised and will enter the millennial kingdom. Though it is mentioned in the same verse, the judgment of the wicked, which is also mentioned, actually occurs a thousand years later as Revelation 20:5 makes clear. At the beginning of the millennial kingdom all the righteous have been raised from the dead, and those living, both Gentiles and Jews, who survived the Great Tribulation will enter the Millennium in their natural bodies and will perform natural functions in that kingdom. Only those who are wicked will still be in the grave and not resurrected.

The New Testament does not detail the characteristics of the millennial kingdom because this is covered in many passages in the Old Testament.

Characteristics of the Millennial Kingdom

Scripture speaks of kingdoms in various forms, sometimes kingdoms relating to this world and sometimes spiritual kingdoms, where God is recognized as the ruler. The millennial kingdom is primarily a political kingdom, though it has spiritual aspects and Jesus Christ is the King of Kings, who has come to reign over the earth. Because it is an earthly kingdom with Christ on the throne, it obviously cannot be fulfilled in the present age when Christ is in heaven, though Christians form a part of the kingdom of God in a spiritual sense.

Jesus Christ will serve as King of Kings and Lord of Lords in the millennial kingdom and will fulfill the promises that He will sit on David's throne over the house of Israel (2 Sam. 7:16; Ps. 89:20–37; Isa. 11:1–16; Jer. 33:19–21). In His relationship to Israel as her king, He was born to rule over her (Luke 1:32–33). The people of Israel rejected Him as their king (Mark 15:12–13; Luke 19:14). In His death it was posted on the cross that He died as a king (Matt. 27:37). It is in keeping with this that when He comes again, He comes as the King who will fulfill prophecies of His ruling over the Davidic kingdom (Rev. 19:16).

In addition to reigning over Israel as the Son of David, Christ is also King of Kings over the entire earth, and this includes, of course, the Gentile world. As Psalm 72:8 states, "He will rule from sea to sea and from the River to the ends of the earth."

The fact that Christ will reign over the entire world is taught by many Scriptures (Isa. 2:1–4; 9:6–7; 11:1–10; 16:5; 24:23; 32:1; 40:1–11; 42:3–4; 52:7–15; 55:4; Dan. 2:44; 7:27; Micah 4:1–8; 5:2–5; Zech. 9:9; 14:16–17). These verses demand a literal kingdom and a literal reign of Christ on earth.

In Christ's reign over the people of Israel, David will be resurrected as king and serve as a regent under Christ (Jer. 30:9; 33:15–17; Ezek. 34:23–24; 37:24–25; Hosea 3:5). The twelve apostles also will have part in the reign of Christ on earth and will judge the twelve tribes of Israel (Matt. 19:28).

The divine kingdom of Christ in the Millennium is clearly over the entire earth in fulfillment of Psalm 2:6–9 (Ps. 72:8; Dan. 2:35; 7:14; Micah 4:1–2; Zech. 9:10). This is in keeping with His title in Revelation 19:16 as "KING OF

KINGS AND LORD OF LORDS." The millennial kingdom will be an absolute rule of Christ, and it will involve judgment on any who oppose Him (Ps. 2:9; 72:9–11; Isa. 11:4).

Righteousness and justice will characterize the millennial kingdom, in contrast to the corrupt governments of our present world. In keeping with this, Psalm 2:10–12 speaks of His wrath, and Isaiah 11:3–5 gives assurance that the poor and the meek will be dealt with righteously. Because all those who enter the Millennium are either resurrected saints or people who have been born again, in the early stages of the Millennium, particularly, there will be a righteous manner of life in the world such as the world has never seen.

The Spiritual Life in the Millennium

Though the millennial kingdom is a political kingdom, it nevertheless will provide a context for a high level of spiritual life and experience. Though Christ reigns in the hearts of His followers now, in the millennial kingdom this will be universal, political, and visible.

An important part of this is the fact that Christ will be visibly present and the world will be able to see His glory (Matt. 24:30). Psalm 72:19 also mentions that the whole earth will be filled with His glory.

In addition to other aspects of the spiritual life, full knowledge of God and His ways are indicated, as stated in Isaiah 11:9: "They will neither harm nor destroy on all my holy mountain, for the earth will be full of the knowledge of the LORD as the waters cover the sea." In contrast to the Mosaic Law, which was written on tables of stone, God will put His truth in the heart of man, and all will know the facts about Jesus Christ (Jer. 31:33–34). God will also forgive their sins and pour out His blessings upon them. The spiritual life in the Millennium will be manifested in righteousness among the saints, who will flourish (Ps. 72:7).

In addition to the kingdom being righteous in relation to spiritual life, it will also be a time of peace, when nations no longer fight each other, and interpersonal relationships will be peaceful. Isaiah 2:4 states, "He will judge between the nations and will settle disputes for many peoples. They will beat their swords into plowshares and their spears into pruning hooks. Nation will not take up sword against nation, nor will they train for war anymore."

In keeping with righteousness and peace, there will be universal joy, as stated in Isaiah 12:3–4: "With joy you will draw water from the wells of salvation. In that day you will say: 'Give thanks to the LORD, call on his name; make known among the nations what he has done, and proclaim that his name is exalted.' "

In keeping with these predictions, the power of the Holy Spirit will work in the millennial scene. Saints in the Millennium will be indwelt by the Holy Spirit, even as they are in the present age (Isa. 32:15; 44:3; Ezek. 39:29; Joel 2:28–29). The millennial kingdom will manifest a high level of spiritual life unequaled in any previous dispensation.

The Millennial Temple

In Ezekiel 40:1–46:24 the millennial temple is described, a huge building rich in spiritual meaning. The spiritual significance of the millennial temple will differ from the importance of the temple under the Mosaic Law, but it will provide a means of worship of God, including animal sacrifices. Though animal sacrifices in themselves do not provide any relief from sin, as was true in the Old Testament, millennial sacrifices will look back to the cross even as sacrifices in the Mosaic period looked forward to the cross. Though some have opposed the idea of animal sacrifices in the Millennium on the ground that Christ's sacrifice was sufficient, there does not seem to be any other suitable explanation of the details of the millennial kingdom and the details of the sacrificial system in the millennial kingdom as provided in Ezekiel. During the present age the Lord's Supper is the scriptural reminder of the sacrifice of Christ.

The Social and Economic Characteristics of the Millennium

The Millennium will also provide a high level of social and economic characteristics for the entire earth. Probably the majority of those living in the Millennium will be saved. Only saved people will enter the Millennium, and those born during the thousand years of Christ's reign will, of course, need to receive Christ as Savior and be born again. Because there is such universal knowledge of Christ and because Satan is bound and cannot oppose this, it would seem that the great majority of those who live in the millennial kingdom will be saved even though at the end of the Millennium there will be a rebellion on the part of those who are not actually saved. The millennial kingdom will also be a time of great prosperity, and there will be no poor people or people suffering from lack of economic needs. The curse on the ground pronounced after Adam's sin will be lifted, and even the desert will produce abundant crops (Isa. 32:14–15; 35:1–2). It will be a time of general prosperity for the entire earth (Jer. 31:12; Ezek. 34:25–29; Joel 2:21–27; Amos 9:13–14).

In the millennial kingdom each of the twelve tribes of

Israel will have its designated portion of the promised land as indicated in Ezekiel 48.

One of the outstanding features of the Millennium is that there will be no war. Accordingly, expenditures necessary to support a military branch of the government will be turned into improvement of the social and economic life in the Millennium.

Contributing to peaceful circumstances, there will be universal justice. As stated in Isaiah 11:4, "With righteousness he will judge the needy, with justice he will give decisions for the poor of the earth."

The earth, which was cursed following Adam's sin, will now bring forth abundantly as stated in Isaiah 35:1–2, "The desert and the parched land will be glad; the wilderness will rejoice and blossom. Like the crocus, it will burst into bloom; it will rejoice greatly and shout for joy. The glory of Lebanon will be given to it, the splendor of Carmel and Sharon; they will see the glory of the LORD, the splendor of our God." There will be abundant rainfall (Isa. 30:23; 35:7).

In general, there will be prosperity under the ideal government of Christ (Jer. 31:12; Ezek. 34:25–29; Joel 2:21–27; Amos 9:13–14).

Apparently, sickness will be less prevalent in the Millennium than in any previous dispensation, and physical difficulties may be healed (Isa. 29:18; 33:24). Even those who are lame will be healed and those who are dumb will be able to speak (Isa. 35:5–6). In general, longevity will characterize the human race, for a person who dies at the age of one hundred will be considered a child (Isa. 65:20).

Because the earth's population has been decimated by the events of the Great Tribulation, those in the Millennium will witness a large increase in the birth rate. In the book of Jeremiah the Lord says, "From them will come songs of thanksgiving and the sound of rejoicing. I will add to their numbers, and they will not be decreased; I will bring them honor, and they will not be disdained. Their children will be as in days of old, and their community will be established before me; I will punish all who oppress them" (30:19–20). The Millennium will be a golden age to a far greater extent than any previous dispensation.

Jerusalem in the Millennium

In the Millennium Jerusalem will be exalted as a city and raised topographically above the surrounding land. According to Zechariah 14:10, "The whole land, from Geba to Rimmon, south of Jerusalem, will become like the Arabah. But Jerusalem will be raised up and remain in its place, from the Benjamin Gate to the site of the First Gate, to the Corner Gate, and from the Tower of Hananel to the royal winepresses." Jerusalem will be greatly enlarged but will include some of the old landmarks such as the Benjamin Gate (Jer. 37:13) as well as other gates (Zech. 14:10).

Any close examination of the many particulars that abound in prophecy of this kingdom on earth will make it clear that these prophecies are not being fulfilled in any sense now and that they require a second coming of Christ, a personal return of Christ on earth, and the establishment of His kingdom on earth for a thousand years before the eternal state begins. The millennial kingdom will not be fulfilled in the new earth (Rev. 21–22), as in the Millennium there will be sin and death and divine judgment as well as other factors not found in heaven. The Millennium will be fulfilled in the present earth, even though some changes will be made in the earthly situation.

Questions

1. To what extent is the doctrine of the Second Coming recognized as a future event in orthodox interpretation of the Bible?
2. What are some of the predictions of the second coming of Christ in the Psalms?
3. How do the Psalms describe Christ's rule on earth after His second coming?
4. What is added concerning the future millennial reign of Christ in Isaiah 11?
5. How does Daniel 7 describe the second coming of Christ?
6. How is the second coming of Christ in Daniel 7 distinguished from His first coming?
7. What does Zechariah add concerning the coming of Christ?
8. To what extent is the subject of the second coming of Christ revealed in the Gospels, the book of Acts, the Epistles, and the book of Revelation?
9. How does the second coming of Christ relate to His ascension into heaven?
10. Is the Rapture ever found in the Bible in passages dealing clearly with the second coming of Christ to the earth?
11. How does Revelation 19 describe the second coming of Christ?
12. How does the second coming of Christ in Revelation 19 contrast to Christ's coming at the Rapture?
13. How does the second coming of Christ differ from the Rapture in regard to the outcome of the clash between Christ and the armies of the world at the time of the Second Coming?

14. What happens to the future world dictator and the false prophet at the time of the Second Coming?
15. What happens to Satan at the time of the Second Coming?
16. How does the prophecy of Revelation 20:1–3 differ from the present state of Satan in the world?
17. Why is it necessary for Satan to be bound to achieve the world situation described in the Millennium?
18. What happens to those who were beheaded for their witness of Christ in the Great Tribulation?
19. What are the martyrs raised to do after their resurrection?
20. How does this prophecy concerning the resurrection of the martyred dead prove that the millennial kingdom is still future?
21. Why is the prediction of the general resurrection of all people at one time in one place contrary to what the Scriptures teach?
22. When are the wicked dead raised?
23. What happens to Satan at the end of the Millennium?
24. What are some of the general judgments on the Gentiles at the time of the Second Coming?
25. What is the general judgment on Israel at the time of the Second Coming?
26. When will the Old Testament saints be raised from the dead?
27. Who will remain in the grave after the Millennium begins?
28. To what extent is the millennial kingdom a political kingdom?
29. How will the reign of Christ fulfill the prophecy of Christ sitting on David's throne?
30. In what respect is Christ King of Kings over the entire earth? How is this supported from Scripture?

31. Why is David raised from the dead? What will he do in relation to Christ's kingdom reign?

32. To what extent will righteousness and justice characterize the millennial kingdom?

33. To what extent is the Millennium also a time of unusual spiritual life?

34. Indicate some of the aspects in which the spiritual life in the Millennium will be different than it is today.

35. What part does war have in the millennial kingdom?

36. Will the millennial kingdom be a time of joy and peace?

37. How is the Holy Spirit related to saints in the Millennium?

38. What is the purpose of the millennial temple described in Ezekiel 40:1– 46:24?

39. How do we interpret the fact that the new temple predicts animal sacrifices?

40. If animal sacrifices are offered, what will be their spiritual significance?

41. In contrast to the millennial sacrifices, what was the meaning of Old Testament sacrifices?

42. Does the fact of animal sacrifices in the Millennium contradict the fact that Christ died and His death is sufficient for all?

43. What are some of the social and economic characteristics of the millennial kingdom?

44. What portion of the earth will the twelve tribes of Israel have during the Millennium?

45. To what extent will the earth bring forth fruit abundantly in the Millennium?

46. What will be the characteristics of sickness and physical difficulty in the Millennium?

47. What will be the population of the millennial earth in view of the fact that people will live longer?

[15]

What Will Heaven Be Like?

The Loosing of Satan and the Final Revolt against Christ

AT THE CONCLUSION of the thousand-year reign of Christ, Satan, who has been bound, will be let loose again, and he will immediately continue his opposition to the things of God by enticing those who were not genuinely saved in the Millennium to follow him in conquering the city of Jerusalem. Though everyone who enters the Millennium as an adult will be saved, it is obvious that as children are born, they have to make a decision to receive Christ. Under the circumstances, in the millennial kingdom all will be required to profess faith in Christ, but in some cases this will not be real, and, actually, they will be unsaved. When Satan is loosed, they follow him and attempt to conquer the city of Jerusalem. This is stated in Revelation 20:7–9:

> When the thousand years are over, Satan will be released from his prison and will go out to deceive the nations in the four corners of the earth—Gog and Magog—to gather them for battle. In number they

are like the sand on the seashore. They marched across the breadth of the earth and surrounded the camp of God's people, the city he loves. But fire came down from heaven and devoured them.

The rebellion is short-lived. And when it is over, the devil is cast into the lake of burning sulfur, where he will be tormented forever (Rev. 20:10). It is significant that the beast and the false prophet who were thrown into the lake of burning sulfur a thousand years earlier are still there and are still under torment.

The Judgment at the Great White Throne

The closing verses of Revelation 20 describe a white throne in space where the wicked dead will be judged. This is revealed in Revelation 20:11–15:

Then I saw a great white throne and him who was seated on it. Earth and sky fled from his presence, and there was no place for them. And I saw the dead, great and small, standing before the throne, and books were opened. Another book was opened, which is the book of life. The dead were judged according to what they had done as recorded in the books. The sea gave up the dead that were in it, and death and Hades gave up the dead that were in them, and each person was judged according to what he had done. Then death and Hades were thrown into the lake of fire. The lake of fire is the second death. If anyone's name was not found written in the book of life, he was thrown into the lake of fire.

As this Scripture makes clear, those who will be raised whose names are not in the Book of Life (the record of those who are saved) will be cast into the lake of fire, which is described as the second death. Though it is difficult for people to believe that this will be literally fulfilled, the doctrine of eternal punishment is just as clear in Scripture as the doctrine of eternal heaven. Accordingly, this passage emphasizes the importance of winning people to Christ and helping them accept the gospel that their eternal destiny might be in heaven.

The earth and sky that characterize our present existence will flee away and be destroyed (2 Peter 3:10; Rev. 20:11; 21:1). According to Revelation 21–22, the eternal destiny of those who are saved will be the new Jerusalem in the new heaven and the new earth.

There is remarkable little revelation given concerning the characteristics of the new heaven and the new earth. All we know about the new heaven is that there will be no sun or moon, and probably no stars (Rev. 21:23–24). The new earth will be illuminated by the presence of the glory of God. Little is known about the new earth, but it apparently is round because there are directions of north, south, east, and west mentioned (Rev. 21:13). There will also be no sea or oceans. The physical qualities that enter into the eternal state differ greatly from what we now experience.

Major attention is focused upon the new Jerusalem which apparently will adorn the new earth. The new Jerusalem will be as beautiful and fresh as a bride, and it will come down from God out of heaven. In contrast to the earth, which is destroyed, the new Jerusalem was apparently in existence in space during the millennial kingdom. Though Scriptures are not clear on this point, some believe that the new Jerusalem during the Millennium will actually be the home of all the resurrected saints as a satellite city, and they will be able to commute to the earth to carry on their earthly functions and then return home to their place in the new Jerusalem. In any case, the Scriptures are clear that the new Jerusalem will be located on earth in the eternal state and be the home of all who are saved.

A great deal of attention is given to the design of the new Jerusalem. According to the Scriptures, it will have twelve foundations, which seems to make sure that it will rest on the new earth. Surrounding the city will be a high wall with three gates on each of the four sides with the gates bearing the names of the twelve tribes of Israel.

The description of the city indicates that it is glorious and brilliant like a gigantic jewel. The size of the city will be 12,000 stadia (Rev. 21:16) or about 1,400 miles, and its length will be the same as its width. It will also be 1,400 miles high.

The city is described as made of jasper and pure gold. The jasper is a different stone than exists today as a jasper because it is said to be clear in contrast to the jasper of today which is opaque. Gold also seems to differ from what is gold metal today because it is pictured as glass so that the light will go right through it. The foundation of the city has twelve stones mentioned, representing every color of the rainbow, and the scene will be indescribably beautiful, being illuminated by the glory of God.

The high wall about the city indicates that only those worthy may enter. According to Hebrews 12:22–24, the new Jerusalem will be inhabited by angels, the church, righteous people in general, and Jesus Christ:

But you have come to Mount Zion, to the heavenly Jerusalem, the city of the living God. You have come to thousands upon thousands of angels in joyful assembly, to the church of the firstborn, whose names are written in heaven. You have come to God, the judge of all men, to the spirits of righteous men made perfect, to Jesus the mediator of a new covenant, and to the sprinkled blood that speaks a better word than the blood of Abel.

The twelve gates in the city, representing the twelve tribes of Israel, are said to resemble a single giant pearl. The streets will be made of pure gold, but transparent like glass, and God is said to give it light (Rev. 21:23). Though the city has gates, the gates will not be shut, but no one will be allowed to enter who is not considered worthy.

In Revelation 22 a river is described with water as clear as crystal, which comes from the throne of God and flows through the city, representing abundance of spiritual life. The Tree of Life, which is described as bearing twelve kinds of fruit, one each month, is on either side of the river, apparently indicating that there will be more than one tree with the river flowing between. The leaves of the tree are for the health, or for the healing, of the nations. As all those who are there have been resurrected, they will not have physical maladies, and the tree simply adds to their health and enjoyment.

Many questions are left unanswered, but Scripture does describe very simply that the lot of those who are saved will be to "serve him" (Rev. 22:3). Our greatest privilege in heaven will be to serve God in some significant role.

The fact that heaven is an ideal place where there will be no tears, sorrow, or death is a great comfort to Christians, some of whom endure much in this life. For the Christian, there is no setting sun but a glorious future of being with the Lord forever. Our final home will be in the new Jerusalem.

Because the future of a Christian is so wonderful, our present task is to tell others that they may partake freely of eternal life (Rev. 22:17). The final note of the book of Revelation is that Christ is coming soon (Rev. 22:20).

Christians living today in a world that is increasingly difficult have the wonderful anticipation that the rapture of the church may occur any day, when they will find themselves in the presence of the Lord to be forever in His joyous fellowship.

Questions

1. Describe the loosing of Satan and the final revolt against Christ.
2. What happens to those who join in Satan's revolt?
3. What happens to Satan?
4. What is the significance of the fact that the beast and the false prophet are still in the lake of fire after one thousand years?
5. What happens to the earth and the heavens when the great white throne is set up in space?
6. What happens to those whose names are not in the Book of Life?
7. What does the judgment of the great white throne indicate regarding the necessity of leading people to Christ?
8. What does the Bible teach about the new heavens?
9. What does the Bible teach about the new earth?
10. What is the significance of the fact that the new Jerusalem is not said to be created but descends from God out of heaven?
11. If the new Jerusalem will be a satellite city over the earth during the Millennium, what is the possibility

that this might explain where the resurrected saints live when they are not engaged in ministry in the millennial earth?

12. How is the new Jerusalem described in general?

13. What are the dimensions of the new Jerusalem?

14. What is the significance of the wall around Jerusalem and the gates?

15. Who will inhabit the new Jerusalem according to Hebrews 12:22–24?

16. What provides light for the city?

17. What does the river described in Revelation 22 represent?

18. How do you explain the tree with its twelve months of fruit relating to the health and well-being of the nations?

19. What, according to Revelation 22:3, will be our function in the new Jerusalem?

20. How do you summarize the fact that heaven is an ideal place for the children of God?

21. In view of the fact that we have such a wonderful future, what is our present task on the earth?

Scripture Index

Genesis

1:1, *27*; 1:2, *37*; 1:27, *x, 45–47*; 2:7, *47*; 2:16–17, *49*; 2:17, *50*; 3:2–6, *49*; 3:4, *xi;* 3:14–15, *50;* 3:15, *19, 49, 51*; 3:16, *50*; 3:17–19, *20*; 3:22–24, *50*; 6–8, *20*; 6:13, *53*; 10, *60, 63*; 10:2–5, *59*; 10:5, *61*; 10:6–20, *59*; 10:21–31, *59*; 11–50, *60, 68*; 11, *xi, 60*; 11:1–9, *60*; 12, *60, 68*; 12:1–3, *20, 53*; 12:10, *64*; 12:10–13, *64*; 12:14–16, *64*; 12:17–20, *64*; 16:1–15, *64*; 16:7, *36*; 18:1, *36*; 22:11–12, *36*; 24:27, *127*; 26:1–6, *64*; 41:1–43, *64*; 41:37, *38*; 41:38–40, *119*; 46:1–7, *64*; 46:28–47:12, *64*

Exodus

3:14, *30*; 4:22, *32*; 12:31–50, *64*; 28:3, *119*; 31:2–3, *38*; 31:3, *119*; 35:30–35, *119*

Numbers

21:6–7, *94*; 21:8–9, *94*; 27:18, *38, 119*

Deuteronomy

6:4, *39*; 6:17, *15*; 25:4, *15*

Joshua

1:8, *16*; 8:32–35, *16*; 21:43–45, *64*

Judges

1:21, *65*; 1:27–28, *65*; 3:10, *119*; 6:34, *119*; 11:29, *119*; 13:25, *119*; 14:6, *119*; 14:19, *119*; 15:14, *119*

1 Samuel

10:10, *119*; 16:13, *119*; 16:14, *99, 102*

2 Samuel

7:16, *184*; 22:31, *16*

1 Chronicles

5:25–26, *61, 65*

2 Chronicles

36:17–20, *63*

Ezra

1:1–2:70, *63*

Nehemiah

1:1–6:16, *63*; 11:1–2, *63*; 5:8, *61*

Psalms

1, *140*; 1:2, *16*; 1:2–3, *135*; 2, *175*; 2:5–9, *175*; 2:6–9, *184*;
2:9, *185*; 2:10–12, *185*; 12:6, *16*; 14:1, *29*; 16:9–11, *144*;
19:7–11, *15*; 22, *14, 176*; 22:18, *14*; 23, *176*; 24, *176*;
51:11, *99, 102*; 72, *176*; 72:7, *186*; 72:7–11, *176*; 72:8,
184; 72:9–11, *185*; 72:17–19, *176*; 72:19, *185*; 89:20–37,
184; 90:2, *30*; 93:5, *16*; 102:27, *30*; 119:9, *16, 134*; 119:11,
16; 119:18, *16*; 119:89–93, *16*; 119:97–100, *16*;
119:104–105, *16*; 119:105, *134*; 119:130, *16*; 139, *31*;
139:7–9, *31*; 145:3, *30*; 147:5, *31*

Proverbs

30:5–6, *16*

Isaiah

2:1–4, *184*; 2:4, *186*; 7:14, *36, 144*; 9:6–7, *36, 184*; 11,
176, 190; 11:1–10, *184*; 11:1–16, *184*; 11:3–5, *185*; 11:4,
185, 188; 11:9, *183, 185*; 12:3–4, *186*; 16:5, *184*; 24:23,
184; 29:18, *188*; 30:23, *188*; 32:1, *184*; 32:14–15, *187*;
32:15, *186*; 33:24, *188*; 35:1–2, *187, 188*; 35:5–6, *144,
188*; 35:7, *188*; 40:1–11, *184*; 42:3–4, *184*; 44:3, *186*;
52:7–15, *184*; 53, *37*; 53:5, *52*; 53:6, *144*; 55:4, *184*;

Zechariah

2:10–11, *177*; 2:12, *177*; 4:6, *38*; 9:9, *184*; 9:10, *184*;
11:12–13, *14*; 14, *177*; 14:3–4, *177*; 14:10, *189*; 14:16–17.
184

Malachi

2:10, *32*; 3:6, *30*

Matthew

1:22–23, *13*; 1:23, *144*; 2:2, *61*; 3:11, *95*; 3:16, *40*;
3:16–17, *39*; 3:17, *40*; 4:14, *12*; 4:14–16, *13*; 5:17–19, *16*;
5:18, *13*; 5:22–29, *16*; 6:24, *121, 130*; 8:17, *13*; 10:1, *108*;
10:1–2, *104*; 10:1–4, *108*; 10:2, *107*; 10:7–8, *108*;
12:17–21, *13*; 12:40, *14*; 13:22, *125*; 15:7–9, *13*; 16:4, *144*;
16:18, *108*; 16:19, *108*; 16:21, *144*; 17:1–8, *73*; 17:22, *144*;
19:26, *31*; 19:28, *108, 178, 184*; 20:18–19, *144*; 20:30, *22*;
21:4–5, *13*; 21:42, *13*; 22:2, *97*; 22:29, *13*; 23:39, *178*; 24,
144; 24:3–25:46, *178*; 24:15, *14*; 24:21–22, *164*; 24:23–27,
158; 24:29–30, *164*; 24:30, *185*; 24:30–31, *171*; 25:1–13,
97; 25:31–45, *171*; 25:31–46, *150, 182*; 26:31–56, *13*;
27:9, *14*; 27:10, *14*; 27:35, *14*; 27:37, *184*; 28:19, *37, 40*

Mark

1:8, *95*; 3:13–14, *108*; 3:14, *107*; 6:30, *107*; 8:31, *144*;
9:2–13, *73*; 9:31, *144*; 10:33–34, *144*; 10:46, *22*; 13:24–37,
178; 13:31, *16*; 15:12–13, *184*

Luke

1:32–33, *144, 184*; 1:41, *120*; 1:67, *120*; 3:16, *95*; 6:13,
107, 108; 9:22, *144*; 9:28–36, *73*; 10:7, *15*; 11:13, *99, 102*;
12:35–48, *178*; 16:17, *16*; 17:22–37, *178*; 17:33, *75*; 18:8,
178; 18:31–33, *144*; 18:35, *22*; 19:1, *22*; 19:10, *73*; 19:14,
184; 21:25–28, *178*; 21:28, *76*

John

1:1–2, *35*; 1:2–3, *46*; 1:3, *72*; 1:4, *72*; 1:10–14, *72*;

1 Corinthians

1:1, *107*; 1:2, *117*; 1:30, *76*; 2:12, *97*; 2:13, *16*; 3:1, *117*;
3:10–15, *154*; 3:11–15, *97*; 4:6, *107*; 4:7, *157*; 4:9, *107*;
6:13–20, *48*; 6:15, *96*; 6:19, *31, 48*; 6:19–20, *74, 98*; 6:20,
74; 7:23, *74*; 9:1, *108*; 9:24–27, *155*; 9:27, *48*; 11:3, *96*;
11:26, *178*; 11:27–30, *123*; 11:31–32, *123*; 12:4–31, *97*;
12:8–10, *105*; 12:9, *110*; 12:10, *109, 112, 113*; 12:12–13,
126; 12:12–14, *96*; 12:13, *52, 95, 96, 98*; 12:28, *103, 104,
108, 110*; 12:30, *110*; 14, *112*; 14:1–4, *109*; 14:1–12, *112*;
14:13–20, *112*; 14:19, *112*; 14:22, *112*; 14:26–28, *112*;
14:26–38, *112*; 14:27, *113*; 14:34–35, *112*; 15:1–3, *144*;
15:7, *107*; 15:24, *34*; 15:45, *97*; 15:50, *148*; 15:51–53, *148*;
15:51–58, *148*; 15:58, *157, 160*

2 Corinthians

1:21–22, *100*; 5:5, *98*; 5:10, *152*; 5:14, *41*; 5:14–15, *79*;
5:17, *94, 97, 153*; 5:17–21, *78*; 5:20, *79*; 5:21, *51, 52, 79*;
8:23, *107*; 11:2, *97, 143*

Galatians

1:19, *107*; 2:9, *107*; 3:2, *98*; 3:13, *75*; 3:26, *34*; 3:27, *95*;
4:5, *75*; 4:6, *98, 128*; 5:16, *118, 124*; 5:16–18, *133*;
5:19–21, *124*; 5:22–23, *126*; 6:14, *125*

Ephesians

1:3, *33, 34*; 1:4–12, *153*; 1:7, *76, 136*; 1:7–8, *84*; 1:14, *76*;
1:22–23, *96*; 2:1, *53*; 2:4–10, *146*; 2:5, *93*; 2:8, *84, 85, 88*;
2:8–10, *84, 90*; 2:9, *89*; 2:10, *89, 93*; 2:16, *78, 96*; 2:18, *34*;
2:19–22, *97*; 3:1–12, *108*; 4:4–5, *96*; 4:5, *95, 96*; 4:6, *34*;
4:11, *103, 104, 108*; 4:11–13, *97*; 4:11–16, *118*; 4:18–19,
53; 4:24, *93*; 4:30, *101, 119, 122*; 5:16, *75*; 5:18, *120*;
5:19–20, *128*; 5:23–24, *96*; 5:27, *148*; 5:30–32, *96*; 6:12,
125

Philippians

2:13, *41*; 2:6–7, *36*; 2:25, *107*; 3:20–21, *48*; 3:21, *148*

2 Peter

1:21, *10*; 2:1, *54, 74*; 2:15, *54*; 3:3–4, *54, 178*; 3:4, *47*; 3:10, *195*; 3:15–16, 16; 3:18, *118*

1 John

1:3, *34*; 1:9, *123, 153*; 2:1, *34*; 2:2, *76*; 2:18, *166*; 2:22, *34, 166*; 2:27, *113*; 3:1, *34*; 3:24, *98, 128*; 4:1, *113*; 4:2, *113*; 4:3, *166*; 4:8, *30*; 4:10, *76*; 4:13, *98, 128*; 5:14–15, *137*

2 John

7, *166*

Jude

14–15, *178*

Revelation

1:2, *16*; 1:6, *97*; 1:7–8, *178*; 2:11, *53*; 2:25–28, *178*; 5:8–9, *74*; 5:9, *74, 136*; 6, *168*; 6–18, *150, 168*; 6:2, *169*; 6:12–14, *169*; 7, *170*; 7:9–17, *170*; 7:10, *89*; 9:7–12, *169*; 9:15, *169*; 12:12, *150*; 13, *67, 163*; 13:1, *163*; 13:1–10, *163*; 13:2, *163*; 13:4, *168*; 13:5–7, *163*; 13:8, *168*; 14:1, *170*; 14:3, *75*; 14:3–4, *74*; 16:1–2, *169*; 16:3, *170*; 16:4, *170*; 16:8, *170*; 16:10, *170*; 16:15, *178*; 16:17–21, *170*; 19–20, *178*; 19:7–9, *97*; 19:11–15, *178*; 19:11–16, *178*; 19:11–21, *178*; 19:16, *184*; 19:20, *179*; 20, *180, 194*; 20:1–3, *150, 180*; 20:4, *149*; 20:4–6, *144, 181*; 20:5, *183*; 20:5–6, *149*; 20:6, *53*; 20:7–9, *193*; 20:7–10, *182*; 20:10, *193, 194*; 20:11, *195*; 20:11–15, *194*; 20:12–13, *149*; 20:14, *53*; 20:15, *55*; 21–22, *189, 195*; 21:1, *195*; 21:8, *53*; 21:13, *195*; 21:16, *196*; 21:23, *197*; 21:23–24, *195*; 22, *197*; 22:3, *197*; 22:17, *37, 198*; 22:18, *16*; 22:18–19, *109*; 22:20, *178, 198*

Topical Index

A

Abrahamic Covenant, 60

Abram, xi, 52, 53, 60, 64
  chosen of God to fulfill His purpose in redemption, 53
  promised blessing to the entire world, 53

Adam
  innocent of sin before the fall, 50
  after fall into sin, radically changed, 50

Adam and Eve, x, 19, 49, 50, 53

Armageddon, 168-71

Assyria, 62, 65, 146

Assyrian Captivity, 62, 63, 65

Assyrian Empire, 65

Atheism, 29

Attributes of God, 29–32

B

Babylon, 63, 65, 66, 146, 161

Babylonian captivity, 63

Bible
  alleged contradictions examined, 22
  claims inspiration, 12–19
  faith in, 8
  hope for the future, 2
  impossible to duplicate, 3
  information about God, 2
  inspired of the Holy Spirit, 8–12
  produced by human authors guided by the Spirit, 12
  proof of, as the Word of God, 8
  provides correction, 9
  reveals truth about God, 9

Other Discovery House books that will feed your soul with the Word of God:

The Christian Salt and Light Company
by *Haddon W. Robinson*

A powerful application of the Sermon on the Mount principles as the path to true happiness.

The Solid Rock Construction Company
by *Haddon W. Robinson*

Writing on Matthew 6 and 7, the author illustrates how Christians can build their lives on the right foundation, how to pray wholeheartedly, serve devotedly, and trust completely.

Daniel: God's Man in a Secular Society
by *Donald K. Campbell*

Intriguing, contemporary perspective and helpful application of the prophecies in Daniel.

Prophecy for Today
by *J. Dwight Pentecost*

A straightforward exposition written with clarity and conviction, this new edition includes added material to make it a complete overview of prophetic doctrine.

Waiting for the Second Coming
by *Ray Stedman*

These studies in Thessalonians provide fresh insights for today's problems and offer a forward look of hope to the certainty of Christ's return. It is full of encouragement for world-weary believers.

The Priority of Knowing God
by *Peter V. Deison* with Foreword by Howard Hendricks

Insights and answers to the challenge of establishing and maintaining a meaningful relationship with God through daily devotions.

Note to the Reader